THE ENABLER NARENDRA MODI

BREAKING STEREOTYPES

MANISH ANAND

Manish Anand

ISBN-13: 97-8151-4145-760

ISBN-10: 1514145766
BISAC: Political Science / Political Process / Leadership

First published in 2015

E-mail: anand.m25@gmail.com

FOR MY SON SHLOK
WITH LOVE

CONTENTS

MANISH ANAND

'I have spread my dreams under your feet;

Tread softly because you tread on my dreams.'

--- William Butler Yeats

Preface

Politics has mostly been the instrument of power in India for ages.

It has even been the most potent change agent in India's history. If Chanakya's feat in overthrowing a decaying Nanda dynasty from the seat of power of Magadh at a time when India faced existential challenge from Alexander "the Great" was an act of individual political craft, later history has shown politics evolving into an institutional process with remarkable abilities to co-opt religion, people and custom to serve larger Indian interests.

The Great Ashoka embraced Buddhism not only as his religious belief but as his statecraft in an instance of the most potent form of marriage of politics and religion. Even after more than two thousand years, Central and South-east Asian nations stay emotionally closer to India because of the statecraft of Ashoka. Later, the great Mughal emperor Akbar revisited his predecessor from India's golden ancient age to replicate the model with an envious success. History is testimony to the fact that whenever politics accepted the social realities and co-opted those who were left on the margins, India saw prosperity with no parallel. And, most importantly, Ashoka and Akbar were not prisoners of past, and had deep contempt for stereotypes. They broke many stereotypes and thought ahead of their times. They were not afraid of consequences of their decisions, which were not liked by orthodox power centres. Besides being great emperors, they were great politicians, and their political statecraft was not constant but ever evolving.

Mahatma Gandhi was another great politicians who astutely sought to mainstream those who had been kept on the margins for ages. His zeal to win over Muslims from the British may have sown seeds for a separate nation, but he evolved the politics of the day for people in true sense to have their voices and in the end handed over a nation in India as had nearly been in the days of Ashoka and Akbar.

The instrument of politics gains much more potency under people who are not slave to the past and have abilities to out-think others, besides thinking ahead of their times. The only permanent is change, and if politics stays constant it can only gift gloom. India after Independence saw politics doggedly refusing to change. Politics over the years was caged, and leading politicians were no more than parrots telling stale tales. The potency of the nation was affected. India struggled to just feed her people. There was no more dreams for the nation.

The Congress was the beneficiary of the goodwill of the people for Mahatma Gandhi. A grateful nation sought to pay the debt to the Mahatma by religiously voting for the Congress. It took almost six decades for the people to unyoke themselves from the Congress.

Narendra Modi rode the wave to walk into 7, Race Course Road, and became the second RSS pracharak (bachelor preacher) Prime Minister of India. Before him, Atal Bihari Vajpayee had flung open the office for the saffron outfit. Vajpayee firmed up the BJP as a reliable alternative at national politics. Yet he could not knock out the Congress. The RSS and Congress are existential foes of each other. Vajpayee over the years had become a centrist due to the uniqueness of his times. In contrast, Modi wears the RSS on his sleeves. In the 2014 verdict, Modi gave near mortal blows to the Congress. The grand old party is left with self-doubts. The journey down the hill for the Congress is not yet over. The Congress leaders are aware that a decade of Modi rule would snap the life support of the party. Modi too is aware of the fact, and accordingly has co-opted regional parties, while keeping the Congress at arm's length. The script of quarrelsome Indian polity with the advent of Modi was written in the 2014 verdict.

Modi government could push a few of the key legislations early in its life only after the President Pranab Mukherjee delivered straightforward message to the Opposition. The voice of sanity lost its audience quickly. And the BJP and Congress are back sparring, while holding the legislative progress of the country hostage their narrow considerations.

It was simplistic to run down Modi magic in 2014 as advertisement blitzkrieg. The popular narrative in India had been hostage to the New Delhi clique. The larger political class of the BJP and Congress, besides the media formed this clique. They stayed unaware of disconnect with the fast changing realities of India. The clique was a prisoner of stereotypes turned into institutionalized group-thinking by the television driven media. The Modi juggernaut left the clique gasping for breath. The clique was event obsessed, and conveniently ignored the depth of change in the society. The yearning of the young India did not blip on the radar of the clique. So, they believed a fractured mandate was on the way, and when faced the reality to the contrary of their expectations they began drumming up the advertisement blitzkrieg narrative.

Large parts of India had heard of Narendra Modi when he was the chief minister of Gujrat. Now, India has seen him in good measures. He arrived in New Delhi on a tidal wave. He struck awe in his foes and friends both. Many months have gone by since his inauguration in New Delhi. And he has been praised and slammed in equal measures.

But even his ardent foes admit that Modi is now perched as an emperor of Indian politics. They state that he has surpassed the stature of Indira Gandhi of 1971 fame when she was India's most powerful leader and had unveiled a single party rule in the country. They also claim that Modi's position is both ominous and providential. His position could be ominous, because he may throttle dissent and cause serious damage to Indian democracy. At the same time, it could also be providential, because he can guide India onto a new path and liberate shackled potential of the country.

Much of the awe against Modi is arguably because India knew only Congress as the political culture. And Modi is India's first non-Congress Prime Minister. It may sound odd, because there were seven Prime Ministers, who headed non-Congress governments. Even Atal Bihari Vajpayee of BJP was Prime Minister for about six years. Yet, Modi is the first non-Congress Prime Minister in the true sense. This requires a little understanding. The Congress in India is not just a political party, but a culture. And that culture was seeded deep into Indian democracy by Indira Gandhi. Her stature was such in her prime time that she ensured Constitution Amendment (42nd) to give India the character of a welfare state. All her successors bore her imprints in their statecrafts. Even Vajpayee was a Congressman in his deeds. Essential character of a Congressman is his remarkable ability to tolerate corruption and stall change. The Congress politicians are popular among the party workers, because they share their spoils in large-hearted manner. They go extra miles to get works of their followers done even if it required bending and breaking rules.

Modi is seemingly an anti-thesis of what the Congress stands for. He's not that king who looks other ways when his ministers indulge in loot. He

3

surely seems against secular corruption. India's secular corruption over the years fattened many vested interest groups, which have roots deep enough to create ripples in society and government apparatus. They have been the unhappy lot after the inauguration of Modi. Loosely, it's said that Modi has shut down many "shops". And on this account he's a lot different than Vajpayee and, hence, a first non-Congress PM of the country.

Indeed PV Narsimha Rao and his Finance Minister Manmohan Singh sought to force open the window of India to the world, which was further carried forward by Vajpayee. But they could not lay their hands on a formidable electoral template. Both were rejected by the people. They suffered from contradictions. They wanted to write new chapters in Indian economy and polity, yet could not shun the ideological imprints of Indira Gandhi fully. Rao was a Congress man, but had vision to think beyond the Nehru-Gandhi bank of ideas. Vajpayee was an RSS man, but had co-opted socialists, who were non-Congressmen for just namesake. Vajpayee was a minister in the Morarji Desai Cabinet. The old man was a hardcore Congress man and a rival of Indira Gandhi. Vajpayee propped up VP Singh as Prime Minister with the support of Left parties. VP Singh had spent his life in the Congress and quit the party to head the Janata Dal, which was essentially a loose confederation of provincial caste chieftains, in a bid to settle scores with Rajiv Gandhi. Vajpayee in his thoughts was centrist, with little leaning to the right. Modi is not Vajpayee and neither has he sought to be one at all. It's not just choice, but because of the tectonic shift in Indian politics after the 2014 Lok Sabha elections.

Modi discovered the politician in him as a chief minister. He does not belong to New Delhi. And, hence, the multi-headed New Delhi caucus may not have spread its tentacles on Modi. India has been held hostage to the interests of the New Delhi caucus (dealt in details in the book). The Congress has been the chief priest of the high temple of the New Delhi caucus. The Congress essentially is a political culture wherein the power of decision making is centralized, known as 'High Command' culture. This bears strong imprints in the statecraft. Even though India is a Union of states, India's statecraft essentially is of centralized planning and decision making. The Centre decides what the states should do. The Centre decides how much money states should spend and for what. The Centre has been a 'Big Daddy' of all the states.

And for that matter Indian Parliament enacting a law on acquisition of land in 2013, which was actually a politically legislation thrust upon the government due to Rahul Gandhi's obsession to do the politics of land, is a case of bone stuck in the neck due to lack of knowledge of the local realities. Land is a state subject and all state governments have their own respective policies or laws on acquisition of land. Then what was the need for the Centre to enact a law and whose amendments Modi is desperately seeking, because he believes it has forced a lock-down on development. If not for Rahul Gandhi ambushing Bhatta-Parsaul village in Greater Noida to throw his weight behind arguably rich farmers of western Uttar Pradesh, India may have continued with the law on acquisition of land made in British time. The Centre essentially lacks trust in state governments. The bureaucrats in New Delhi believe the states need to be monitored, else they will 'eat' the fund sent from the Centre. Modi in his deeds has shown that he has deep contempt for such belief.

Additionally, the Congress culture embraced all political parties because of its singular feat in leading majority governments. The non-Congress governments have never been of a single political party and even the Janta government was coming together of two contradictory political groups of socialists and saffronites swearing to diverse ideologies. Modi heads an NDA government, which in action is largely a one party government, with allies working under the scanner of his sharp eyes.

So, Modi is a non-believer in the politics of poverty (dealt in detail in the book). The Congress, socialists and Left swear by the politics of poverty. This culture essentially is distribution of wealth, centralization of decision making, and sycophancy. Through the welfare core of the statecraft, Congress envisaged distribution of wealth among the poor directly. This subsequently birthed politics of poverty. But the collateral damage to Indian ethos was in the form of rampant corruption which spread its tentacles in all walks of lives. The mode to distribute wealth to the poor fell prey to the cunning crop of teeming millions who had connections everywhere to pocket at least half the money sent by the Centre. They infected the political class, judiciary, police, and civil society with their vice. And they gave as an end result birth to a corrupt society. Vajpayee should not be counted among the non-Congress Prime Ministers purely for the reasons that he was clueless to clamp down against corruption and the centralization of decision making exercise. Other six Prime Ministers – Morarji Desai, Choudhary Charan Singh, VP Singh, Chandrashekhar, HDS Deve Gowda, and IK Gujral -- were either from the Congress having crossed over to other parties in search for greener pastures or were propped up to the post as part of the trick game of the grand old party.

Modi struck within two months of his inauguration demolished the high temple of the politics of poverty – Planning Commission. All chief ministers as a matter of religious duties would seek sanctity from the high priest of this temple for their annual budgets. Modi as chief minister had seen the bigotry of snobbish priests of this temple where he came each year to reject the stereotypes of many priests who were sanctified to be beholder of all knowledge. Modi inaugurated NITI Aayog wherein chief ministers head sub-groups on various subjects. Now, the chief ministers have become the priests of the ghostly abode of erstwhile Planning Commission presiding over the functions of the NITI Aayog.

But most importantly Modi assured people from the ramparts of the Red Fort, that he would 'neither take bribe nor allow others to do the same (naa khaaoonga, naa khane doonga)'. No Prime Minister before him acknowledged the cancer of corruption in such a manner and owned up responsibility to crush it down. Now that the economy has resumed its journey on the upward trajectory, the battle against corruption has left the realty sector bleeding, which joyously was a beehive of black money all these years. Real-estate prices in Delhi and satellite towns around have slumped by at least 20 per cent after the inauguration of Modi. The tap of black money appears to have been turned off and there is tangible effect on the grounds. And for self-explained reasons property dealers and those have invested in properties are the ardent Modi baiters.

But the question foremost in the minds of political pundits is whether Modi will win another election or not. His statecraft is not yet electorally tested. Most immediately, Rao and Vajpayee were the reformers in true senses who were rejected by the people. In their times India came under the firm grip of Maoists. The Red Corridor dotted India right from the border with Nepal to deep forests of Chhatisgarh and further down in Andhra Pradesh. The Government of India officially admits 80 districts in the country being in strong grip of the Maoists. The Left Wing Extremism spread its influence among the poor tribal and Dalit, because they stayed on the margins and the economic growth, which surpassed nine per cent mark in Vajpayee's time, left them untouched. They could not access those benefits on which the Central government spent billions of dollars each year. Such programmes were subverted by a well-oiled nexus of political class, middle men, bureaucracy, and the police. The last high priest of the Planning Commission Montek Singh Ahluwalia slightly revised Rajiv Gandhi's famous assertion, that only 15 paisa of one rupee sent by Centre reached the people. Ahluwalia said the amount actually was (after three decades of Rajiv Gandhi's statement) 16 paisa. Yet, all governments have been obsessed with the idea of the welfare state. They were so, because it suited them politically. Reforms unveiled by Rao and Vajpayee created the oasis of prosperity, leaving large contingent of darkness for majority of the people. Modi won a historic majority, because he promised to light up this dark-continent (dealt in detail in **Herd Breaker**).

Modi is arguably a non-believer in the idea of India being a welfare state. He has run down Mahatma Gandhi National Rural Employment Guarantee Act (MGNREGA) in Lok Sabha in a manner suggesting his contempt for such schemes. Under him the state has taken a definite turn from the path of welfare activities to one of an enabler for people to avail benefits of the fruits of development and become partner in the growth. He talks of mass movements for all his pet slogans. And, naturally, in the case of most of UPA flagship welfare schemes, Modi has not yet dust-binned, but has showed least zeal in implementing them. So, the National Food Security Act awaits light of the day.

In place Modi has launched several social sector schemes to empower people living on the margins. But in none of them the state is directly contributing anything. Be it Jandhan Yojna, or Pradhan Mantri Bima Yojna or for that matter Atal Pension Yojana, the basic criteria to avail them is to contribute even if the amount is meager. And, thus, Modi has donned the robe of an enabler and seeks to create platform for people to come and join with their own money and get benefits of the schemes.

Modi, incidentally, leads India at a time when demography has changed substantially. Half the population is less than 30 years of age (average age of India in 2015 is 27 years). His ambitious plans for 'Skilled India' and 'Make in India' are outcomes of demographic challenges. He knows that welfare measures of yesteryears would not make any meaningful interventions in the lives of the youth. They want a new deal. In Modi, they sensed a rare opportunity to make an electoral choice to break free from shackles of self-limiting social and economic conditions. Modi is now an emperor of Indian politics, because he broke the caste and community herds, who by habit and conditioning participated in elections in stereotyped manners. Modi broke many stereotypes and he has to consolidate and further cement his political path (dealt in detail in **Dream-walking**).

By 1971 Indira Gandhi was perched as an empress of Indian democracy. She had established a political cult with no parallel. After about six years of flux in Indian politics, she had unveiled a one party rule. And her cult grew manifold, after she ran her surgical knife on Pakistan. She midwifed birth of Bangladesh with surgeon's precision. And in the process she lifted the doom from the conscience of millions of Indians who suffered collective national depression following India's humiliating defeat at the hands of mighty Chinese army in 1962. The Opposition quite deservingly, hailed her 'Durga (symbol of Shakti, power)'.

Destiny could not have been more kind to Indira Gandhi. She was blessed with absolute power. Many saw in her India's resurgence. She seized the opportunity to effect fundamental changes to Indian democracy and economy. And, thus, the Indian democracy got the twin legs of secularism and socialism. Pandit Jawahar Lal Nehru had groomed her politically and ideologically. He shaped his daughter's worldview. Incidentally, destiny was much kinder to her, for she not only grew in the bosom of Nehru, but also under tender guidance of Mahatma Gandhi. Nehru was an internationalist and also the father of industrial India. But his daughter was a case in contrast. She was more of a nationalist. Her father co-opted industrial world. She shunned them. Her father knocked at the doors of United Nations for solutions to vexed Kashmir issue. She cared the least for any international power. She was uncluttered and shunned lures to romance an international stature.

In her statecraft, Indira had Mahatma Gandhi's imprints and not of her father. She anchored her politics on the plank of anti-poverty measures. Nehru dreamt of large industries and equitable distribution of wealth. But she was no believer in large industries and the free market economy taking care of the poor. She unapologetically disowned Nehruvian model of economy and instead unveiled direct transfer of wealth to poor and nationalization drives to become the queen of Left.

Indira incidentally had to carve out her space when a galaxy of stalwarts not only within Congress but also outside confronted her. If K Kamraj and Morarji Desai were her challengers in Congress, she had to politically outweigh leaders like Jayaprakash Narayan, Charan Singh, Atal Bihari Vajpayee, and George Fernandes in the Opposition. Modi now is seen as a blend of both Nehru and Indira. He's more fortunate than Indira politically. Modi admirers would like to believe Modi has the best of Nehru and Indira in him. Yet, Nehru, lest be forgotten, was a democrat even admired by his foes. Modi has not yet shown that spark to be hailed a democrat in Nehruvian sense. Indira institutionalized sycophancy in the Congress and the government wings. Modi also has shown this frailty to savour acts of sycophancy.

Napoleon Bonaparte was once asked if he preferred an able general or a lucky one. The legendary warrior said that he always preferred a lucky general. Modi's luck is envious. In a party, which appeared mired in fratricidal war over leadership only a few years ago, Modi appears to have no challenger. He equally has no challenger even outside his party. His nearest rival as far as stature is concerned is Nitish Kumar, who has been chief minister of Bihar for almost a decade. But Kumar's story does not go further, because he does not have a party to play a role in national politics. He has to indulge in politics of arithmetic, which by its very nature is self-limiting. Modi has been lucky that the global oil price meltdown came at a time when he assumed office. The oil price by all indications is for lower level for a longer time. Modi and state governments have sought to fatten their purses by jacking up Central and state taxes on retail oil sale. Modi's predecessor Manmohan Singh's second innings (UPA-II) was wreaked from the burden of the runaway oil prices, leaving a trail of cascading effects on all walks of lives.

A major exodus of leaders in Congress awaits the elevation of Rahul Gandhi to the post of party president. Quite a good number of Congress leaders with mass base are in touch with leaders of Janata Parivar for political partnership in future. Birth of a few more regional parties on the lines of NCP of Sharad Pawar is not ruled out. The Congress is staring at an uncertain future, as untested Rahul acolytes take reign of the party from the old brigade. There surely is further bottom for Congress to slip into.

However, Modi has challengers who are seeking to grow in their stature. Arvind Kejriwal is one of them who hit the national headlines as a phenomenon. Yet, he is a king of politics of muck and carries strong self-destructive streak in his personality to stay long in politics. The Congress is the natural choice for regional parties to flock to for a non-BJP alternative. And, the Congress has a remarkable ability to stage a comeback when the party is ruled out by all. It did make such a comeback in 2004. The Congress is a natural choice of the poor. Modi swung them on his side by selling them a dream. But if the dream fails to take the wings of reality, they will not lose much time to go back to the party of their natural choice.

No Gandhi scion had to struggle for power for such long time as had been the case with Rahul. Even after 11 years of Parliamentary career, he is not sure of his position in Indian politics (dealt in detail in **The burning house**). And this speaks enough for Rahul and his abilities. His grandmother turned Congress into a Left and he along with his mother Sonia Gandhi further turned his party into more Leftist than even the Left. It's to the credit of the mother and son duo of Congress that the architect of economic liberalization Manmohan Singh proved an anti-thesis of his self in his decade long reign as Prime Minister of India.

Still, Modi has shown his bold, brazen, and bulldozer streak of his leadership after his inauguration in the middle of 2014 (dealt in detail in **Brazen bursts**). He is fairly accused of centralizing power in the Prime Minister's Office (PMO). He keeps hawk's eye on performance of all ministries. He appears paranoid of elements which forced lock-down on the Manmohan Singh government. His government has gone after Non-Governmental Organizations (NGOs) with vengeance, besides unveiling National Judicial Appointment Commission to clip the wings of the judiciary. His government has treated the crop of NGOs with disdain.

That he developed cold-feet in jolting the great Indian bureaucracy from age old inertia is quite evident. Modi gave Ajit Seth two extensions. Seth actually served tenure of four years in place of two as initially decided. Modi has two of retired babus -- Nripendra Mishra and PK Mishra --

heading the great bureaucracy in the PMO. Modi's image has been of an agile and active leader, but bureaucracy under him is the same dull, lethargic and idea impoverished entity. Modi did not challenge babus, but has co-opted them. In his singular bid to keep a tight lid over his ministers, Modi has turned bureaucrats more stubborn to change for the better. Modi is no different from his predecessors when it comes to dealing with the bureaucrats.

It's to the credit of the deep roots of bureaucracy that the idea to bring talent from outside in the government has been a non-starter. Railways continue to be a top heavy bureaucracy, while trains run late by hours. Ministries are not yet debugged from the virus of drafting letters. Ministers in the Modi Cabinet barring a few have allowed the bureaucrats an autonomous zone, being wary of the fact that their Prime Minister has a zest of dealing with the babus directly.

And most importantly not much is heard of 'Damad ji'. No promised actions against him in Rajsthan happened despite the BJP coming to power there. Modi and Vasundhara Raje Scindia had told people not only in Rajsthan but across the country umpteen times about the unscrupulous land deals involving Robert Vadra (son-in-law of Sonia Gandhi) in the state. Yet, people do not know what was unscrupulous about those land deals (dealt in detail in **Turning of wheel**). And for this reason, Modi is naturally accused of having co-opted elements of the New Delhi caucus.

This book tells the story of Modi through the people on the grounds and seeks to address the larger issue of the politics of statecraft. The RSS, which is the mother bank of ideology of the BJP, does not believe in personalities. Modi is an out and out RSS man. The RSS flows in the veins of Modi. He owes his oratory and candour to the RSS. And the RSS believes in process and not events. Modi has unveiled the process of change, which is not big-bang in nature but subtle. This book does not look the advent of Modi as an event, but a process. The enabler Narendra Modi has broken many political stereotypes and many others wait being demolished. Because millions of poor have kept their faith in Indian democracy even though not much had been done for them and the time is now to pay back for their undiluted faith in the idea of India.

The book -- *The enabler Narendra Modi* – goes beyond events, and shares insight, anecdotes, and perspective behind the tectonic shift in Indian politics. Besides the book attempts to reveal facets of the man of the moment, whom his rivals call 'emperor of Indian politics'.

The enabler Narendra Modi

New Delhi Caucus

IN 2010, a highly resistant bug was named after New Delhi.

The bug is immune to any anti-biotic. It's accounting for deaths, whose causes are hidden by hospitals, in big numbers. The government of the day was predictably furious when such a bug was named after the national capital of the country. Popular anger sadly does not change the reality, and the bug stays quite potently in big hospitals much immune to high dose of disinfectants sprayed regularly. Hospitals are clueless on ways to eliminate this bug and have reconciled to their fate to live with it.

The all resistant bug may have been given a name in 2010, but New Delhi has stayed a mecca of corruption for decades and suitably immune to any crackdown. The scale of corruption has been such that a monumental ghetto rose in its vicinity in the name of Gurgaon, the millennium city, which among its all attributes is famed for absorbing the black money poured from across the country. Gurgaon has been the dump yard of national black money.

New Delhi is a city of deal-makers. From the comforts of Lutyens' zone and its expansion, the political class embraces the vested interests of the business world, with those from the media acting as middlemen. They are the constituents of the New Delhi caucus. Bureaucrats are the most powerful spokes of the wheels of the New Delhi caucus. The wheels run and run to pocket the wealth of the nation for a tiny lot, who subvert the aspirations of the people for change. This caucus stays alive beyond the public scrutiny and long arms of the investigative agencies. That this hydra-headed monster has held Indian democracy hostage to its vested interests is proof enough of the fact that the New Delhi Caucus has roots too deep to be uprooted any time soon.

India is a prisoner of the New Delhi caucus. It's such a powerful block which prevents change in the country with ease. They thrive with attitude of status quo. This caucus stands on twin legs of bureaucracy and the political class. The middle men, judicial functionaries, Non-Governmental Organizations (NGOs), business men, top echelons of media and opinion makers are multiple organs of this New Delhi caucus. They serve interests of each other and protect them from any threat. Their roots are so deep that no government, including the one headed by Narendra Modi, has touched them in any inimical manner. They survive because interests of many powerful entities are embedded in them.

The New Delhi caucus historically ensured that all wings of the government were headquartered in the national capital. Many of them should not have been in New Delhi, including for instance headquarter of Indian Navy. There is no merit to plethora of public sector units based in New Delhi. They could have easily been in areas of their operations. The Railways has thousands of babus perched in Rail Bhavan. Many of their siblings are perched in various other Bhavans in state capitals. Their inhabitants are essentially file carriers drawing fat salary and perks. Even while India chugs along on rugged tracks, they are firmly perched in the comforts of the national capital.

Gopinath Munde was killed in a tragic fashion in a road accident at a round-about near India's most powerful address -- 7, Race Course Road. He died within months of the inauguration of Modi. Munde was a mass leader and BJP's sole face in rural Maharashtra. His followers did not lose much time to cast aspersions on Munde's immediate political rival within the BJP in the Maharashtra politics-- Nitin Gadkari. The air was so warm with conspiracy theory that Modi gave his nod to a CBI probe into the mishap, which from the outset was a routine road accident in which millions of Indians lose their lives each year. Munde's death killed Gadkari's prospects to lead Maharashtra where his party soon came to power.

Gadkari would soon set out to overhaul the Motor Vehicle Act and ask his bureaucrats to study the best international laws. Such studies are essentially pretext for foreign tours. But when Gadkari pressed for an early draft on amendments to Motor Vehicle Act, the babus did what they had been doing for ages. They 'copy pasted' provisions of laws prevalent in Canada, France, England and elsewhere. So, a fine of $100 was plainly converted into corresponding value of rupees and rounded off to a lump sum figure. The bureaucratic inertia is such that this 'studied' draft bill passed the scrutiny of top echelons of babus and the minister without an eyebrow raised. It was only when his ministry was hit by scores of public feedback highlighting impractical nature of the law, that the legislative proposal invited close scrutiny of the minister. Much time has passed since Munde's death, but not a word has changed in the Motor Vehicle Act.

Modi unveiled 'Make in India' and 'Skilled India' campaigns. But irony of the irony is that they are being manned by those who have least expertise in any of the two domains. The most unskilled bureaucrats are expected to herald a generation of skilled people. No wonder that even after a year in the office, they are mere campaigns, with little to show on the ground. Yes, the babus are visiting the foreign capitals to know the latest know-how, as they had been doing for ages. Those already in the consumer businesses are showing themselves of having contributing in the 'Make in India' campaign. The 'Make in India' campaign is obsessed with the idea to attract large scale business units from developed world. They would come if they want to and if assured of the market. Campaign or no campaign, they would purely be driven by their hardcore business interests.

The New Delhi caucus is a big threat to the very idea of 'Make in India' campaign. Government is the biggest buyer of goods produced by the business houses. In the next five years, the Modi government would seek to spread the power transmission lines and reach electricity to millions of homes across the country. Billions of dollars would be spent in the gigantic exercise. This will also offer opportunity to entrepreneurs to tap the opportunity. But will the massive scale of public spending help incubate the next generation of entrepreneurs in the manufacturing sector. The answer is a clear no, because the New Delhi caucus would never allow them, because they would pose direct threat to those already in such businesses.

Tendering is the major tool to help the next generation of entrepreneurs to come on the horizon. 'The norms of tenders are such that someone starting a business despite possessing the technology and ability to set up a unit to manufacture the goods at locations of demands would not qualify to become part of the exercise,' said one such corporate executive, whose entrepreneurial ambitions stay blocked with the web spread by the New Delhi caucus.

Tenders incidentally are drafted at instances of business houses, who know ways to grease the palms of decision makers. Tenders would be accordingly drafted to protect their interests. The ways of tendering despite the fact the government has embarked on digital ways of doing so has ensured that a new generation of entrepreneurs never came up in the manufacturing sector even though they have made the world to acknowledge their talents in the services sector.

'I was being pressurized by a vendor to clear a project. I would be asked to clear the file by even chairman of the railway board. Yet, I did not heed to their pleas. The vendor would ask what was stopping me from clearing the file when his share is guaranteed. From bottom to top, all were given cuts by the vendor. I did not clear the file and I was shunted to an insignificant posting. No meaningful postings in Railways happened without bribing the superior. Now, I have come to railway board as a member after the change in government, which was a position sold for decades,' said a railway board member.

It's not just railways but all wings of the government where posts were up for sale for decades. Those with connections with political class would ensure plumb postings for themselves. Bureaucrats and political class have been in a happy marriage, with each taking care of interests of the other. They have such a holy relationship, that the bureaucrats never retire, as many governments ensure many avenues wait for them after they superannuate from their services. New Delhi has a plethora of bodies, which have functions for namesake, but act as abode for retired babus to live off life of luxury at the expense of tax-payers' money. Those who take good care of their political masters become Governors and lieutenant governors of Union Territories on their superannuation. They hold their relations of 'I scratch your back and you mine' sacrosanct. Only a few of the bureaucrats have stayed away from this New Delhi caucus and made significant contributions to nation building.

The North and South Blocks overseen by the majestic Rashtrapati Bhavan as a routine always hosted industrial honchos who could walk into the offices of the custodians of the Finance Ministry with ease and without leaving any record. They could walk into the office of the Finance Minister any time and any day. If the Finance Minister were not to be in his office, he would host the industrial leaders at his residence for late night meetings. On one such occasions an appointment of a delegation of journalists with the Finance Minister, who now occupies an eminent position, was cancelled because one of India's biggest businessman had suddenly appeared there without prior notice. Such practice was not just confined with the Finance Ministry, but covered all key ministries having industrial interfaces. The power of New Delhi caucus was such that the coal-blocks during the UPA times were allocated to business houses engaged in making of underwear, vests, toothpaste, and so on. The business men could know exactly what government planned to do about key assets and the manners of taking policy decisions in advance.

This act of 'sneaking in' the offices of powerful ministers by corporate honchos stopped forthwith after Modi assumed power. The bureaucrats too were warned not to entertain such visitors and the message was understood in quick time. Yet, the New Delhi caucus is still alive and not exactly crushed by all the might.

All cities in India have embraced vertical growth and allow constructions of high rise to meet the increasing demands for habitations. New Delhi is a case in contrast. The national capital has roughly 26 square kilometers of Lutyens' zone where India's 'high class' lives in one storey houses with acres of lawns for them to walk through in morning and evening. Peacocks and monkeys give good company to the blessed politicians. The hypocrisy is such that millions of people in Delhi live in sub-human conditions on periphery of the national capital in ways which would be nothing short of living on the edge and at threat of being consumed by any form of disaster. It's not only members of political class who are perched in such aristocratic habitations, as they share the space with their siblings from bureaucracy, judiciary, army, navy, and air force, besides the whole army of retired babus holed in the comforts of nests of democratic decorations of various commissions. The hypocrisy of India being a welfare state is laid bare each day to those who cross lanes and by-lanes of Lutyens' zone.

Many rags to riches stories have been scripted in such holes in the Lutyens' zone. One such beneficiary is now a three time MP of Lok Sabha, who was known as a loafer in a small city, but a stroke of luck made him to stay as a 'helping hand' to a pracharak of the RSS, who called shots when Vajpayee was the Prime Minister. In just about five years, he had assets in the form of farm houses, besides becoming a member of the Lok Sabha later on. His wealth is such that he could afford to take hundreds of guests in charter planes to his native place for a family function. His tribe thrives in New Delhi and has many siblings in many political parties.

The New Delhi caucus put excessive roadblocks to the 2010 Commonwealth Games preparations. They tested the patience of the then Sheila Dikshit government at each step. Delhi Urban Arts Commission (DUAC) is one such spoke in the great wheel of the New Delhi caucus. This body of architects who sought to keep Delhi as the British had left would thwart any move of the Sheila Dikshit government to get infrastructure in place to address the needs of the times. In 2006, AK Walia, who was the then PWD minister of Delhi wanted to unveil the next phase of construction of flyovers in the national capital to unclog the city. His plans did not move an inch, because the cheer-leaders of the heritage 'wallahs' would not compromise a bit.

The matter would come to such deadlock that a critical flyover to facilitate the smooth travel of the Commonwealth Games athletes from the Games Village on the Yamuna bank in East Delhi to Jawaharlal Nehru stadium in South Delhi would remain on the files moving back and forth. Exasperated by elements in the New Delhi Caucus, Sheila Dikshit had to meet the then Prime Minister Manmohan Singh to get the roadblocks removed and the clearance came so late that the Barapulla flyover could be completed in the shoddiest manner with just a few days to go for the prestigious event to kick off. This flyover is now a lifeline for millions of commuters who come and go out of Delhi each day and is now choked in peak traffic times. A similar elevated corridor to link east and western parts of Delhi was shelved by the frustrated Delhi government, after repeated pleas for clearance from the savior of art did not yield any result.

It's to the credit of this New Delhi Caucus that those who hit the road to catch a flight in the national capital are sucked by serpentine traffic jams. Delhi government wanted to make the stretch of Nehru Place, which is Asia's arguably largest hardware market, to the airport signal free. But the elements within the New Delhi Caucus who lived in areas of Vasant Vihar had issues about flyovers eclipsing their 'kothis (bungalows)' and came forth with studies claiming that such infrastructure made people in the area depressed and suicidal. Additionally, the 'Malai Mandir' was patronized by one of the occupants of the Rashtrapati Bhavan, who put his feet down against a flyover disturbing the landscape of the south Indian temple. Demands of the commuters fell on deaf ears and now there is a long serpentine line each morning and evening on the stretch giving nightmarish moments to the people.

The New Delhi Caucus has held Indian democracy hostage for decades and not much questions have been asked either. There are 795 members of Parliament in Lok Sabha and Rajya Sabha altogether. Each of them believes that he or she is a lawmaker. But they are not, as they have never been the law makers in true sense. The laws are made by bureaucrats and the so called law makers only approve them following the party whip. A long term Parliamentarian Rashid Alvi, who is a Congress leader, believes that the MPs work like clerks when it comes to making laws. 'It's the bureaucrats who make laws and MPs literally as clerks approve them. The practice is unchallenged,' Alvi said.

It was only the Anna Hazare agitation, which challenged the status quo in making of the laws. He sought to break the practice and for the first time a street agitation influenced drafting of a law in the form of Lokpal. He inspired one more piece of legislation for the unorganized sector of workers, which was enacted by the Parliament subsequently. A five term Lok Sabha MP Devendra Yadav said that the members of Parliament realized quite late that even street agitations could initiate making of laws. It will be pertinent to ask how many laws were initiated by MPs and which actually got approval of the Parliament. Are the MPs really representatives of the people or their roles have been hijacked by the bureaucrats who stay yoked to psyche inbuilt in them by the British? It's no wonder India is a country of laws and rules, and people have least respect for them.

Even the idea of a political party issuing whip to its members in the Parliament should be seen as undemocratic. In the times of Rajiv Gandhi, laws were made in such manner that members of Parliament had to be slaves to 'high command' culture of their respective party. In the form of anti-defection law, members of Parliament were turned into herds. It's common practice for political parties to issue whip to its members to vote in either of the ways on any legislative proposal in both the Houses of the Parliament. This has robbed all sheen of Parliamentary debate. Members of Parliament argue the case of any legislative proposal as if they were school kids and participating in a debate competition.

The Anti-defection law -- The Constitution (Fifty-second Amendment Act) -- was enacted in 1985 when the Rajiv Gandhi led government was perched in Parliament with a brute majority. Yet, he had to get such an undemocratic law passed within one year of assuming office speaks volume of the scale of insecurity that he was blessed with. He commanded much larger mandate (1984) from the people than that of Narendra Modi (2014). Congress had won 414 Lok Sabha seats in 1984 out of the total strength of 543. Yet, Rajiv thought of enacting an anti-defection law within one year of being in power.

One year of Rajiv in office and the same of Modi would make for quite contrasting case studies. Rajiv was a globetrotter and would spend most of the times abroad. He bulldozed Parliamentary democracy for fear of his government being sabotaged from within. His singular act of getting the 'The Constitution (Fifty-second Amendment Act)' turned members of Parliament into 'clerks'. This tool became so convenient for any political party that they have not allowed any discussion on merits and relevance in today's context. Modi has been slammed by Rahul Gandhi for being a globetrotter. Rahul must have been a regular companion to his father when he undertook almost the same number of foreign trips in his first year of office in an era when India had neither liberalized its economy nor had embraced globalization. But the convenient amnesia is the most common attribute of the constituents of the New Delhi caucus.

Three decades have passed by since the anti-defection law was enacted. But no popular scrutiny has yet been allowed on this law. If the purpose was to ensure stability of the government, why could it not be applied only in cases when there would be trust or no-trust vote in Lok Sabha or state Assemblies? It is important to note that the law is being loosely and freely used by political parties to curb the very free thinking of members of Parliament in their positions as true law-makers and stop them to critically scrutinize legislative proposals drafted by bureaucrats.

No wonder the clerks in Parliament treat MPs with disdain. Members of both Lok Sabha and Rajya Sabha admit that the bureaucracy in Indian Parliament is most stubborn and corrupt. They are non-transferable. And, so, they stay true to the maxim -- familiarity breeds contempt. They frustrate MPs to clear their TA (Transport Allowance) claims, besides making them sweat if they have to list questions to raise during Question Hours.

'A Lok Sabha MP had gone abroad as part of the delegation accompanying President during a bilateral visit. He had come to New Delhi to join the delegation from his hometown. But when the TA was claimed, the babu just sat over it and would deny it for months on the grounds that it should be claimed with the President's office,' said an aide of a chairman of one of the Parliamentary committee. The MP knew why his TA claim was not being cleared and asked his aide to give whatever the clerk wanted, he said. But the aide was equally stubborn and well informed about the Parliament and its practice. He wrote a letter to the head of the department, saying that the Parliament consists of President and, hence, the TA claim should be cleared by his office. It was cleared. But majority of MPs do not have aides like him and they have apparently no answer to the ways of well-entrenched bureaucracy of the Indian Parliament.

Such is the power of New Delhi caucus that it has even Indian Parliament in its grip. If an IAS officer can come to the Centre after long stints in states, why not the constituents of the Parliamentary bureaucracy by spending considerable times in state Assemblies? Why should not there be an integrated bureaucracy right from the level of state Assemblies to Indian Parliament to truly reflect the character of Indian society? Why should the bureaucracy in Indian Parliament be directly recruited? New Delhi caucus has ensured that even after six decades of India's freedom the basic reform right in the temple of democracy has not yet been attempted. This is because doing so would disturb the fiefdoms of a few people and also a fine balance, and, hence, the status quo prevails.

Clerks and stenographers have been powerful spokes in New Delhi Caucus for decades. The political class makes them their shadows and the business world co-opt them as partners. Essar leaks have shown the murky nexus of clerks and stenographers with the business world. The beauty of New Delhi caucus is such that a clerk in Government of India could become vice-president of a corporate entity. They are convenient conduits for political class and business world to enter into partnerships. Some of them grew to legendary status having mastered the art of hawala routing of the ill-gotten money of the political class and became inalienable parts of their aka in politics. Staying shadows for long times, they get to know too many secrets and become more than a family member, who could not be hurt.

Over the years, they become partners of the political leaders. They could barge into their rooms without knocking. One colourful anecdote was shared by one such aide. He had barged into the room of a Union Minister in Shastri Bhavan for sharing some information with him. He saw the minister red-faced, with a young woman clutching to her cloths hastily rushing to the washroom. Yet, the minister was all humble and allowed him to share what he had to, while looking all the times to the woman who made desperate attempts to hide from the sight of the visitor. The aide was himself embarrassed and excused himself soon. They shared excellent relations, which lasted even the end of the tenure of the minister.

Tales of stenographers since the days of Indira Gandhi have been legendary. But what is unique is that the clerks and stenographers wielded disproportionate power by becoming shadows of leaders of Congress and socialist parties. The BJP somehow is not yet afflicted by their influence in a manner to draw close scrutiny. Yet, the party is not totally immune to New Delhi caucus.

A private assistant of a key minister in Modi Cabinet had been pestering a vice-president of a large corporate entity for jobs for the followers of his boss. The miffed corporate executive asked the PA to get a few of his men into railway jobs and after that he could consider his pleas. The PA did not understand the underlying message. He kept pestering the corporate executive, who lastly warned him not to call again, else he would take action. This minister is a first timer and his PAs are seemingly novices and yet to learn the art of New Delhi caucus.

Those who know Ram Vilas Paswan would know that RP Rathi is his shadow. Rathi was a lower divisional clerk. Paswan is a beneficiary of the political awakening of the scheduled castes (Dalits) in his home state of Bihar. Incidentally, Paswan wanted to become a police officer. He had cleared the recruitment examination for posts of inspectors. But he failed or was 'failed' in the interview. Later, he cleared the examination of deputy superintendent of police (DySP). Pleased with his performance, his father gave him reward of Rs 100 with which he bought a bicycle. When he was feted for having become DySP people in his areas asked him to plunge into politics and that was late 1960s when castes in Bihar were becoming politically conscious. He took the plunge and got Rs 1000 by his political senior in the Samyukta Socialist Party to contest the bypoll. He was elected to Bihar Assembly in 1967.

Paswan is blessed with an envious sense of political opportunism and has been a crossover in politics, breaking breads with all the colours of politics. Rathi has been his companion since he became a minister for the first time in 1989 in the VP Singh government. Old timers among the stenographers would say that Rathi, who hails from Haryana, has an excellent skill to network and raise funds. So, he is not just a personal shadow of Paswan, but a key functionary of his party -- Lok Janshakti Party.

The Bihar Dalit leader again became a minister in the Modi Cabinet, after his filmstar-turned-politician son Chirag Paswan salvaged his political career by persuading him to join the BJP led NDA just on the eve of the 2014 Lok Sabha elections. And as a matter of right or habit, Rathi's name appeared on the nameplate as an OSD (officer on special duty) of Paswan. But the nameplate had to be taken off in a matter of few days only.

Modi was aware of the elements within New Delhi caucus before he took the oath of the office of Prime Minister. Under his instructions, Department of Personal and Training (DoPT) issued order, saying those who had been in the personal staff of a minister in last 10 years could not be considered for similar positions in the current government. Not only Rathi but many of his tribe were barred from the high offices by the order. The Modi ministers thought that the order could have been routine and on their own appointed their cronies in their personal staff. But soon they were asked to fall in line. Paswan would lobby for Rathi to such an extent that he would go to the Cabinet Secretary Ajit Seth to get an exemption for his shadow, but would have to return after being told that Prime Minister would have none of them with any minister in official positions. And, thus, Rathi as well as some others of his tribe saw their nameplates removed from the corridors of power.

New Delhi caucus fattens on India's politics of subsidy. There is a lot of money on the table by virtue of politics of subsidy for elements of New Delhi caucus to take home. Fertilizer subsidy is one such avenue. Ever since the green revolution, Indian agriculture has been a net abuser of fertilizer. Excessive usage of fertilizers in Punjab is turning the land infertile so much so that the rich farmers of the state are looking at opportunities to buy soil from fertile land anywhere in the country. Barring Tamil Nadu and Gujarat no states in India ever paid any attention to test the health of soil and empower farmers with knowledge for adequate usage of chemical fertilizers.

Foodgrains over the years have turned toxic, besides the ground water. Cancer is the new epidemic in India. People in Punjab, Uttar Pradesh, Bihar, and Maharashtra are becoming cancer patients in fairly large numbers. Yet, no government sought to conduct any empirical study on agricultural land to establish the cause and effect relationship between the toxicity of grains and critical diseases of consumers. It was never attempted because, New Delhi caucus was aware of the fact that a lot of money is at stake in the business of fertilizer subsidy. The fertilizer companies co-opted the media long back to block most of the critical writings on their modus operandi. Modi from the ramparts of the Red Fort admitted that urea meant for farmers was being diverted to chemical companies, and, hence, neem coating is now mandatory to stop such practice.

Modi most eloquently informed the nation in his maiden speech in Lok Sabha, while responding to the discussion on President's address, that his government would arm the farmers with the knowledge of the health conditions of the soil. The farmers would know whether his land needed chemical fertilizers or not and even if it was needed than in how much quantity. He vexed eloquence on the importance of organic farming on a large scale. Despite Modi's penchant for soil testing, the initiative is progressing at snail's pace. In place, the Modi government through the public-private-partnership (PPP) mode would be kick-starting the sick urea unit at Sindri at an investment of $1 billion and another unit in Assam. Clearly, he is seeking more fertilizer production, without doing much of the ground work to cut its consumption. Modi is yet to challenge the New Delhi caucus, which is well entrenched in the fertilizer subsidy business, while not much attention is being paid to the growing health hazard.

India is a large food consumer market of billions of dollars' of worth. But if one were to sneak into the offices of the food safety authorities in state governments, he would be alarmed to know that the people are literally at the mercy of manufacturers of consumable goods. For more than two decades the kids of the country have grown up eating Maggi and now reports are pouring of high lead content, besides taste enhancer beyond permissible limits. The food safety authorities in Uttar Pradesh and Uttarakhand lifted samples of Maggi only after massive campaign against the product in the social media. If one were to take the example of Delhi, the department of food safety has been on perennial staff crunch to carry out even the basic operations. If such is the situation of Delhi, one can imagine the fate of their siblings in state governments. At the national level, there is Food Safety Standards Authority of India (FSSAI), which essentially is a toothless body. It's wholly to the credit of the New Delhi caucus that no deterrent authority has been put in place to take on unscrupulous elements taking consumers for a ride.

There is a whole army of NGOs who in cahoots with celebrity lawyers take recourse to the tool of public interest litigation (PIL) to serve their vested interests. Policy lobbyists abound in the national capital that have on their payrolls retired bureaucrats and eminent lawyers to push cases of corporate entities. The Niira Radia tapes and subsequent investigations into the Essar Leaks revealed the well-entrenched cartel of the New Delhi caucus, which has significant inroads in the media as well. Opinions are on sell, because the New Delhi caucus has significant influence in television and print media. The cancer of paid news is just another powerful spoke in the giant wheel of the New Delhi caucus.

Dr Harsh Vardhan was most admired by Modi for his contributions to the health sector and more particularly for his exemplary deed in eradicating polio from India. He is a sober man and known for spotless character. He had jumped to Modi side when he was not yet in the reckoning to lead the campaign for the 2014 elections. Vardhan was suitably rewarded when the Modi government was inaugurated. He became the Union Health Minister. Vardhan is a passionate campaigner against the menace of cigarette. He did not lose much time to launch a massive campaign against smoking. He wanted exorbitant taxes on cigarettes. He began asking state governments to impose hefty value added tax on cigarette. He favoured fulsome use of pictorial warning. He was a man with the mission. But before he could get his feet moving, he was shunted to a nondescript ministry of science and technology and ministry of earth sciences. Not that his new ministries are of least importance, but the manner in which he was shunted out of his first love where he could have made contribution is a subject of speculation. The needle of suspicion points to the lobby of the New Delhi caucus, which ousted him to release the pressure on the cigarette companies.

Modi has gone after a few elements of the New Delhi caucus in his clean up drive in the administration. But he has not yet gone full throttle against the big shark of the New Delhi caucus. India cannot go full steam until the New Delhi caucus is fully dismantled.

The 56-inch war cry

Octtober 27, 2013 will always remain etched in the mind of Narendra Modi.

The much awaited Lok Sabha elections was still seven months away. The winter had not yet set in and the weather was quite pleasant. The air was warm with excitement. The iconic Gandhi Maidan in Patna was full to capacity, with people spilling over to its periphery. They hummed political talks. The belief that the change was round the corner struck people in good measures. Modi for them was not just a politician, but panacea for all the ills that the country was afflicted with. People perched on every inch of the iconic Gandhi Maidan believed that Manmohan Singh had sold the country to the thugs and all those who were against Modi were essentially crooks.

Bihar must be considered political capital of India. And Gandhi Maidan in Patna has historically been auspicious host for change in Indian politics. There may not be bigger ground than the Gandhi Maidan in the country and to have a capacity crowd is a matter of pride for any politician.

People were brought from nook and corner of the state. The whole BJP machinery had worked for months to mobilize people to come to Patna. And they came in trains, buses, tractors and even trucks in good measures.

Bihar is a state where people are never short of time. Barring jobs in government departments, people in the state do not yet have employment in the sense known in other states. The state is highly fertile, with land blessed by two mighty rivers – the Ganges and Kosi. And the two rivers account for various tributaries. Even though the government in New Delhi never thought to bring canal irrigation to Bihar, people in the state did not complain because waters were always in plenty around. The people of the state have enough time to form opinion on various subjects and most importantly on politics. Each and every word printed in newspapers would be devoured even if they talked of news in China or France. No state in India would be as opinionated as is Bihar and its people highly aware. Even if a graduate of Delhi University may struggle to tell the name of India's Vice-President, school going children in villages of Bihar could tell who the President of China is.

By the time Modi sought to launch his campaign to oust Manmohan Singh from the seat of power in New Delhi from Gandhi Maidan in Bihar, people in the state were pregnant with thoughts that the country had been looted for a decade under the UPA rule. Otherwise also Bihar has no love for Congress, the principal party of the UPA. The people in the state rejected the Congress lock, stock, and barrel two decades away. This party is so dead in the state that days are not far when a tomb for it may be laid in the capital for people to offer flowers for having produced giants of Indian politics in yesteryears. So, tales of misdeeds of the UPA government quite easily magnified in proportion as people hummed politics. They believed UPA to be a demon worthy to be slayed by Modi.

Narendra Modi flew in to the Patna airport in the morning on that day. The airport is very small and close to the heart of the city. The airport is so close to Gandhi Maidan that people perched there could see the jet of Modi flying low for landing. The sight of the jet set off feverish humming crowd to burst into roar loud enough to scare foes of the BJP.

Modi was received at the airport by his party colleagues Rajiv Pratap Rudy and Shahnawaz Hussain. Both were former civil aviation ministers and held permanent entry passes to airports. Local MLA Navin Nitin was with them. The reception was not joyous, but tense. The festivity of the Gandhi Maidan crowd had taken a different course just a little while away. The mood had turned somber. The script had gone a little haywire. Modi saw gloomy eyes of his hosts perspiring on a morning when winter was knocking around. He was then chief minister of Gujrat and faced maximum threat, and was the most protected leader within the political class. He had come for a 'Hunkar' rally at Gandhi Maidan to launch his seven months long campaign to capture power in New Delhi from the Congress.

Scores of Muslims were killed in communal riots in Gujrat after burning of a train in Godhra. Sixty four Gujratis coming back from Ayodhya were burnt to death in the train. Modi was alleged to have not acted strongly enough to stop the carnage of Muslims. He was accused of being a 'silent spectator' to brutal killings of Muslims. Even the barb of 'masterly inaction' was thrown at him. Terror groups took his name often and mentioned post-Godhra riots as alibi for bomb blasts at various places in India. Subsequently Modi became the most guarded political leader in the country.

That day the security protocol of Modi was clearly breached. Bombs after bombs exploded in and around Gandhi Maidan. Some of them went off at Patna Railway station. There was a design in the manner in which the bombs went off in a city where per square inch human density is without any parallel. The bombs were of low intensity and sought to scare and panic people to stampede. Larger design was to tear apart Modi script to launch his campaign to seat of power in New Delhi before it even began.

By the time Modi touched down at the Patna airport, BJP leaders and the police were aware that terror had laid a siege to Gandhi Maidan. That the BJP's Prime Ministerial candidate had just air-dropped into the trap laid by terrorists allowed by local state leadership who seemed looking the other way. If Modi made a hasty retreat, the popular message of him being a coward would have rung across the country. If scores of people were killed in stampede, he would have earned the wrath for having played with the lives of his followers. Even if Modi himself may not have been direct target of terrorists, the design surely sought a mayhem. They sought stampede in the crowd after low-scale blasts set in panic. Accordingly, Modi was briefed about blasts at the airport. Gujrat police chief and BJP leaders advised him to fly back. The risk was high. After patient listening, Modi excused himself to a wash-room. After a while he emerged out and asked for a glass of water. Gulping it in one go, he patted at Rudy and asked him for his vehicle. 'Let's go to Gandhi Maidan,' he told his hosts. He slipped into the front side seat of a white ambassador, which is said to have not even been bullet proof. Seven bombs had gone by the time Modi reached the venue.

From Income tax round-about to Gandhi Maidan, Modi's car went through a sea of people lined on both sides of the road. The security protocol was thrown to the winds. He could have been an easy target. He was in the state whose chief minister Nitish Kumar was his sworn political foe. After about eight years of sharing power with the BJP, Nitish Kumar had snapped ties with the saffron party when he became certain of Modi taking up the leadership of his ally.

Nitish's distaste for Modi had been legendary. He took extra pain to make sure he was not seen with Modi at official functions. He was avoided being photographed together. At some time during those days, Modi went into a washroom at Vigyan Bhavan in New Delhi where a meeting of National Development Council, which is attended by all chief ministers and addressed by the Prime Minister, was underway. Nitish was already inside the washroom. He did not come out of the washroom until enough time had gone by for Modi to have gone back into the main auditorium. He knew photo-journalists would have been camping outside to catch them for those rare snap. Such was the zeal of Nitish not to get photographed with his foe and to run into him that he bothered least about civility lest Muslims in his state pick signals inimical to his political calculations. Nitish's distaste for Modi was beyond political considerations.

The apparent security lapse on that day when Modi sought to sound the election bugle from Nitish's backyard left enough scope for conjectures. In all fairness, however, Nitish was caught off-guard. He may not have anticipated such a turn of events. He regularly briefed Sushil Kumar Modi, who was commanding the crowd at Gandhi Maidan, about incidents taking place. Sushil Kumar Modi is the face of the BJP in Bihar and was deputy chief minister of state with Nitish for about eight years before the two parties parted ways. He told the people not to panic. He attributed loud blasts to tires and fire-crackers going off. An ashen-faced, Nitish later told that six people were killed and 85 others were injured in eight bomb blasts that day.

The immediate motive was to sabotage the 'Hunkar (roar)' rally. Bravery is essential feature of a leader and Modi was tested that day for his nerves. The face of another Modi – Sushil Kumar – told the story of pain and agony. He looked ashen-faced. He knew what all had happened. But he held his nerves and steeled himself. His poise averted a major human tragedy and loss of lives. He ensured that people did not panic. Modi was the only declared candidate for the post of Prime Minister of any political parties. Nitish was an undeclared Prime Ministerial candidate for a non-Congress and non-BJP alternative. He believed that the BJP would never get a majority of its own in the Lok Sabha and the post-Godhra image of Modi would scare away the potential allies for the saffron party. Nitish knew that the Congress would have no choice to back a loose federation of regional parties led by him to stop the BJP from forming the government. He had made moves thinking the onset of political instability in New Delhi. He was aware that his credentials as a chief minister of a state where he had turned around things which had gone messy made him a leader in the same league as was Modi.

Modi and Nitish had common political ambitions. They wanted to be India's next Prime Minister. Both were chief ministers, with records of re-elections under their respective belts. Both were hailed by the media for good jobs done in their respective states. Media portrayed both as good administrators. Nitish was hailed by many, including a few within the BJP, for being a PM (Prime Minister) material. Modi was politically untouchable because of the taint of the post-Godhra riots and his subsequent branding as a hardened 'Hindtutva' hawk.

In contrast, Nitish was an acceptable face for smaller political parties. His distaste for Modi was primarily for the fact that he posed a direct threat to his ambition. His steadfast efforts not be seen with Modi at any of the public fora was for the reason that such an encounter could send adverse message to Muslims in Bihar. Nitish knew that he needed to win maximum number of Lok Sabha seats in Bihar to stand any chance to fulfill his ambition. He needed en-mass support of Muslims in the state. He believed that the Muslims hated Modi for post-Godhra riots (2002) in Gujrat. He knew that there would be slugfest among various leaders of socialist blocks to become next Prime Minister. Hence, he needed a big win in Bihar.

With bombs exploding around, Gandhi Maidan was to deliver a verdict on the road ahead for two contenders for the post of India's next Prime Minister. Not by design, but by a chance, Gandhi Maidan would become an arbiter of their abilities. What happened that day in Gandhi Maidan would weigh high in the minds of the people seven months later to make electoral choices. Modi was aware that Bihar was not a state receptive to the politics of 'Hindutva'. The state was backward, and people voted invariably on caste lines. A better caste arithmetic packaged with the agenda for development stood better chances to outsmart the constituents of the socialists in the state. Modi also knew that his image of a 'Hindutva' hawk was relevant only in Gujrat. India is too large for a parochial leader. The time had come to shed the skin. And it was time Modi slipped into the skin of a man of development.

Modi sought to re-invent himself as the mascot of development. He knew well that to become a Prime Minister he had to step into the shoes of Vajpayee. He knew well the sorry tales of his mentor LK Advani's disastrous 2009 campaign to unseat Manmohan Singh from the power in New Delhi. Hence, Modi looked for a platform bigger than the 'Hindutva' laboratory in Gujrat. But Nitish wanted to bury him in his post-Godhra riot image of a 'butcher' of Muslims. The fight of perception was bitter and fought fiercely in the next seven months. Many regional satraps shared thoughts of Nitish about Modi. Mamata Banerjee, chief minister of West Bengal and Trinamool Congress supremo, would tell journalists during a relaxed chit-chat later, with tea and snacks in abundant supply in the lawn of the official bungalow of her party colleague Mukul Roy, that she would not support a 'dangai (rioter)' face if there were to be a fractured mandate in the 2014 Lok Sabha elections. She would monitor scribes served well the Hilsa fish steam roasted and packed in banana leaves along with dry mutton chops. The tea and snack meet called by her is actually more than a full meal for people from any region in the country. She believed Modi was a 'dangai'. She had pinned hopes on Nitish stopping the Modi march.

On that fateful day every inch of Gandhi Maidan was taken away by the people who had not left the place even after injured were taken away to hospitals. The brave people of Bihar stayed firm on the ground. Modi spoke for about an hour. He did not betray any signs of weaknesses. He unveiled his vision for India. It was development of all and a new deal for India. 'Hindus and Muslims have to decide their common enemy,' he asked and answered himself, that it was poverty. 'It's poverty and both the community have to fight it,' he said. With this slogan, Modi sought to co-opt Muslims in his scheme of things. His agenda for development included the Muslims. Not Many Muslims were present in the iconic ground, but the message spread loud and clear in quick time.

With Muslims constituting sizable political constituency in Bihar, Modi indulged in plain-speaking about them. They had voted for political parties swearing in the name of secularism for many decades as herd, but their lot had remained miserable. The Manmohan Singh government appointed Sachchar Commission in its report had noted that the conditions of Muslims in the country were worse than even the scheduled castes. Modi asked Muslims not to be electoral slaves of political parties. He had taken on Nitish in his den. Seven months later Muslims would not vote for Modi, but his name did not elicit hatred but debate. Muslims were not as acerbic about Modi as Kumar had desired. The script was changing and changing fast to leave the players of the political chess searching for ideas to match the opponent.

In contrast to Nitish's hopes that the post-Godhra riots in Gujrat would destroy Modi campaign, Muslims were ready to discuss him even if they were not yet ready to vote for him. Muslims began discussing their economic conditions in a political context. Still, they sought to defeat the BJP as their principal electoral aims, but the intensity of hatred was diluted. Even if the Muslims did not become Modi cheer leaders, the message from Gandhi Maidan reached the ears of the backward castes that the time had come to unyoke from the socialist parties.

By the time sun set in Patna, full scale of serial bomb blasts was known to the people. Intelligence agencies attributed blasts to Indian Mujahiddin. Nine live bombs were found in a lodge in neighbouring Ranchi in Jharkhand a few days later. Darbhanga module of the Indian Mujahiddin was seen behind the terror act. It emerged that Nitish as chief minister of the state had not been effective enough to crack down against several sleeping cells of Indian Mujahiddin. That such a serial blast took place right under his nose in Patna gave a telling blow to Nitish's administrative skills. He was locked in an electoral contest, which was still building up, with Modi, who was hailed as an able administrator and for having acted tough against sleeping cells of the terror groups in Gujrat.

After an ashen-looking Nitish sought to wriggle out of the blame of security lapse on part of the state government with meek explanations, people began loudly talking about him having allowed the state to lapse into lawlessness. India had been wounded many times till then in various terror attacks. But Bihar was not yet on terror map. People there reacted with horror that terror groups had spread their tentacles in their backyard. By calming nerves of people in Gandhi Maidan and ensuring that no anti-Muslim sentiment ensued following serial blasts, Modi scored a tactical gain over his rival.

Modi was seen to be a brave leader. He had not skipped Gandhi Maidan. He took risk and went there. He oversaw peaceful conclusion of 'hunkar' rally. No stampede took place. Ironically, Nitish did not go to Gandhi Maidan to assure and empathize with agitated people after the blasts. In the aftermath of the serial blasts, it emerged that Nitish lost his campaign plot much before it actually kicked off. He went into a shell. Modi emerged a leader higher in stature by several notches. They were no more equal in the eyes of the people. Modi won the battle of perception at Gandhi Maidan.

Ripples of Gandhi Maidan event would soon spread over to many parts of the country. Politics is above all an art of managing perception. Modi had demonstrated his leadership and had successfully shed the image thrust upon him by stereotyped commentaries about his roles in the post-Godhra riots. He was now the mascot of development. He had shed the skin.

Leap of faith

INDIA'S fame as a golden bird spread far and wide under the reign of Mughal emperor Shahabuddin Muhammad Shah Jahan alias Shah Jahan.

Even with much weakened eye sight he stayed firm in the seat of power. But his rule (1626-58) also saw the most gruesome fratricidal war of succession. Abul Muzaffar Muhi-ud-Din Muhammad Aurangzeb alias Aurangzed Alamgir ascended to power (1658-1707) after putting to sword Shah Jahan's preferred heir and his eldest son Dara Shikoh in the most brutal manner.

Even while Aurangzeb had put to death all royal loyalists, the story goes that Shah Jahan did not give up and ordered mighty doors of Red Fort in Agra be shut. Aurangzeb laid seize to the majestic red-sandstone fort, which oversees the iconic mausoleum known to the world as love poetry carved on marble – The Taj Mahal. The river Yamuna flow nearby. The river is a pale shadow of its historic majesty, after being robbed off waters by hydel dams built upstream. Aurangzeb adopted the strategy to smoke out the inhabitants of the Red Fort. He cut off all supply lines of drinking water to the fort. After a few days when the stock of drinking water inside the fort was over, thirsty old monarch ordered the gate opened and pleaded with his son for a drop of water to quench his thirst. The war of succession was settled by matters of thirst. Aurangzeb ascended to the peacock throne to rule India with an iron fist for 49 long years.

Mughals were immediate predecessors of the British in India. They left lasting impression on the statecraft and politics of India. The BJP not a party headed by a political dynasty slipped into a succession war after the iron grip of long and stable leadership of Atal Bihari Vajpayee and LK Advani loosened. Vajpayee had retired from politics after his health deteriorated. He's in a state where he struggles even to recognize people, while conversation even modest is out of the realm of possibility. Advani in contrast is not only healthy and active but mentally as sharp as ever. But he's on the wrong side of age even by the much liberal yardstick of Indian politics in which 50 years old are reckoned to be young. Advani earned his chance in 2009 to take a shot at the coveted post of India's Prime Minister. India was not enthused. People chose to stay with Manmohan Singh for another five years.

The RSS sensed the demography change of India and its consequences for political class much ahead of others. India was getting younger. The BJP should connect with the youth and reap the demographic dividend. And, so, the RSS prevailed over Advani to slip into the role of a mentor and hand over the mantle of leadership in the party. A reluctant mind works overtime to scuttle demand for change. Advani, incidentally, is older to senior most in the RSS. The RSS had known that the New Delhi caucus of BJP leaders stood no chance to uproot deep roots of the Congress in India. Advani preferred his acolytes Sushma Swaraj and Arun Jaitely for leadership in Lom Sabha and Rajya Sabha respectively. The RSS was not convinced with the choices, but did not press the matter further. In the course of a few years afterwards, the BJP seemed an ineffective Opposition to the UPA, which increasingly got mired in scams after scams. The BJP looked wayward and toothless. It failed to bite and connect with the people. Political pundits did not rule out the possibility that the UPA could pull out a spectacular third win in a row and India could have UPA-III in power.

Advani had built the BJP from the scratch. Even while Vajpayee was the face of the party, it was Advani who toiled for the organizational expansion. When VP Singh embarked on the course of social engineering by implementing the Mandal Commission report for reservation for other backward castes in jobs and educational institutions, Advani sought to carve out a larger political space for the BJP by mounting onto a Rath (chariot) to espouse the cause of building a grand temple at Ayodhya for Lord Ram. He emerged out of the shadow of Vajpayee and changed the course of political discourse. He transformed 'soft' Hindtuva championed by the BJP till then into an 'assertive' one.

He was convinced that the mainstream politics of secularism in India was hollow. Hindus nursed historical grievances due to excesses of Muslim rulers who preceded Mughals. The 49 years long reign of Aurangzeb despite having largest number of Hindus in his army is recorded in history as most adversarial rule of Muslims by the majority Hindu population in the country. The statecraft evolved by emperor Akbar (Abdu'l Fath Jalal ud-din Muhammad Akbar, 1556-1605) in which the majority community was co-opted was abandoned by embracing orthodox elements in Islamic clergy. Advani's rath yatra brought popular scanner of evidences of Muslim excesses against Hindu temples in public discourses. Communal riots were reported from places in Uttar Pradesh, Bihar, Gujrat and other states. Communal tensions were the norms during those days.

Advani transformed himself into a historian narrating tales of medieval India. People at various places where his rath covered heard tales of one -- Mir Baqi – having demolished a Hindu temple at Ayodhya and built a mosque in the memory of first Mughal emperor Babur (Zahir ud-din Muhammad Babur), who ruled parts of North India from 1526 to 1530. Advani advocated use of modern technology to shift Babri mosque from the birth place of Lord Ram to elsewhere so that a grand temple befitting the Hindu sentiment could be built. His campaign communally surcharged North, Central and Western parts of India. Advani would always call Babri mosque a 'structure' since Muslims did not offer prayers there. Besides, Advani raised other issues, including over-turning of the Supreme Court verdict on Shah Bano by Rajiv Gandhi led government to illustrate his idea of 'pseudo-secularism' practiced by the Congress.

Advani's famous rath yatra from Somnath in Gujrat to Ayodhya, which was cut short at Samastipur by the then district magistrate RK Singh, who is now a BJP MP in Lok Sabha, paid rich electoral dividends to the BJP. Subsequently, the BJP sniffed power and in a few years first RSS pracharak (bachelor-activist) would be sworn in as Prime Minister of India. Though Vajpayee became Prime Minister, BJP workers knew that it was Advani who had turned their party into an alternative to the mighty Congress. Advani was not rewarded proportionate to his political achievements. He stayed in the shadow of Vajpayee.

Later, the RSS got tired of Advani, as he sought to re-invent himself to become an acceptable face suitable to compulsions of coalition politics. Vajpayee headed an NDA government with participation of as many as 23 political parties. Advani believed that the BJP's numerical peak had reached and in immediate future the possibility of the party having its own strength to form a government was remote. Vajpayee was aging and looked faltering. His episodes of 'falling asleep' during conversations became legendary tales. Advani had to slip into Vajpayee's shoes fast. His desperation to become Vajpayee came in the form of his sudden discovery in Islamabad that the founder of Pakistan and Muslim League leader Muhammed Ali Jinnah was a secular leader (2005).

It may have slipped out of Advani's mind that Jinnah was very much a fresh character in Indian history, and his deeds of political opportunism in exploiting religion to break India was a central narrative of modern history in the country. By the time Advani's flight touched down at New Delhi airport on way back from Islamabad, a furious RSS told him to step down from the post of the party president. In the scheme of things of the RSS and as part of its indoctrination of cadre, Jinnah is a villain in the modern Indian history who fooled Gandhi and Nehru to cut the limbs of the 'mother land'. The RSS cannot bestow dignity to historical villains, and those from its ranks doing so would only betray the idea of having outgrown the mighty organization. And, thus, despite commanding a sharp memory, Advani blundered by under-estimating wrath of the RSS by giving a new spin to the Jinnah story.

No tree grows under a banyan tree and same held true for the BJP. The RSS had no option but to allow Advani to take the reign of the party again. Later, the RSS allowed him to claim his dues to the organization, as he was projected official candidate for the post of the Prime Minister from the BJP and its alliance – the NDA. But to the misfortune of Advani, he made all the right noise on issues of black money and price rise, but ran into strong wall of unusual popularity of Manmohan Singh, known as an honest man seeking to save the Indian economy from upheavals taking place in the western world. People comprehensively rejected Advani in the 2009 Lok Sabha elections. Advani sang songs whose script did not connect with the electorate.

At last, the RSS nudged Advani to pass the baton to Swaraj and Jaitely for the role of leader of the Opposition in Lok Sabha and Rajya Sabha. The curtain came down on Advani's leadership. The RSS slotted him for a role of a guardian, knowing well that it was a mere façade. The RSS is a 'Big Daddy" of the RSS and no one can outgrow it. Swaraj and Jaitely were not seen beyond the high walls of Indian Parliament. They did not galvanize the BJP cadre. They allowed the Opposition space to be shared by others and even to allow the birth of a political party consisting of NGO activists and media personnel in the form of Aam Admi Party right under their nose. With elections lurking around, the BJP was yet to settle leadership issue. Even after the Congress led UPA delivered bouquet of scams, the BJP appeared far from being seen as coming to the power.

Leaders within the BJP sensed that only Modi could uproot the Congress from power and they began deserting the guardianship of Advani. Jaitely felt the soothing western wind within the BJP firs and switched loyalties. The RSS was convinced that the BJP had to be led by someone from outside New Delhi. It first brought Nitin Gadkari. He was made chief of the BJP, but had to leave the post in an unceremonious manner because of his business interests. The RSS benignly allowed Modi to build his subtle campaign to win the perception both in the party and among the people. In the intervening years Advani had transformed from godfather of Modi to his detractor. With Rajnath Singh as the BJP chief, Advani's isolation was complete within the party. He was condemned to the fate of a sulking old man whom none listened.

With about a year to go for 2014 Lok Sabha elections, national executive meeting of the BJP in Goa chose Modi as the chief election campaigner. Advani took recourse to theatrics and quit from all positions within the BJP. The Congress leaders thoroughly enjoyed the spectacle, with its Ministers quipping 'Lage Raho Advani ji, hum aapke saath haen (stay firm Advani ji, we are with you)'. Advani assisted by Swaraj sought to persuade the RSS chief Mohan Bhagwat to stop the inevitable by producing all the arguments against Modi, but for no avails. Nitish did a world of good for Modi's march to New Delhi. In June 2013, he snapped ties with the BJP. The event cleared ways for Modi to become face of the BJP for elections a year later. After the electoral verdict, a top leader of the JD (U) would confide, that Nitish helped the cause of Modi. Advani showed that he was not yet ready to accept reality as seen by many within the BJP. He held on to his personal grudges.

Many recalled famous gaffe of Manohar Parrikar, who was chief minister of Goa, in which he had called Advani in his trademark 'off the record" conversations with scribes a 'rancid pickle'. Even after a decade of the episode, Advani seems not to have forgotten it. Now that Parrikar is Defence Minister, Advani would slip into back rows in the Lok Sabha if he sees Goa leader sitting in the front row. On one such occasion, JP Nadda and Rahyavardhan Rathore, both ministers in the Modi Cabinet, failed to persuade Advani to go to his seat in the first row where Parrikar was sitting oblivious of the grand old man refusing to come near him. Later, a written note was sent to Parrikar in which he was apparently requested to get Advani to his seat. Consequently, Parrikar went up to Advani and the BJP patriarch relented. Advani had developed similar grudges against Modi when he sensed his design to launch himself into a national leader and sought his blessings.

Ironically, Advani had lost touch with the changed political reality, which, however, was much evident for leaders in other parties. Vijay Bahadur Singh, an MP in 15th Lok Sabha from the ranks of the Mayawati led BSP, was convinced much before the BJP chose Modi as party's candidate for the post of Prime Minister, that the Gujrat chief minister could be a game-changer. 'If Narendra Modi were to be the PM candidate, Uttar Pradesh will be sharply polarized and the BJP may cross its highest tally from the state seen during the peak of the Ayodhya movement.' He was of the opinion that the BJP would not need even to fall back on the 'Hindutva' line and Modi's name would be enough to scale previous peak of the party in the state. The BJP at its peak had won 50 Lok Sabha seats from Uttar Pradesh and ever since had been on the decline to the extent that it had become the fourth party in terms of number of Parliamentary constituencies won from the state.

Perception matters most in politics and without Modi the BJP was not seen as a serious contender for power. The BJP looked tired and fatigued. The party needed fresh ideas. People had developed fatigue for politics around 'Hindutva'. The BJP led coalition government under Vajpayee was seen having done the least for the Ayodhya temple. The era of 'Hindutva' politics was over. In 2012 Uttar Pradesh Assembly elections, Lallu Singh of the BJP lost the poll from Faizabad constituency, which includes the temple town of Ayodhya, after a gap of over 20 years. People in Ayodhya rejected the BJP and elected Tej Narayan Pandey alias Pawan Pandey, a young leader of Samajwadi Party, who promised to develop the area.

Modi had read the wind of change correctly by 2012 and began transforming his image into one of an able administrator who meant business. He talked of big ideas. Various Vibrant Gujrat summits helped him transform his image. Sooner, the BJP president Rajnath Singh acknowledged the ground reality. He brought the succession war in the BJP for leadership to a logical end. He declared at a packed newsroom at the Ashoka Road office of the BJP that Modi would be the candidate for the post of Prime Minister. The BJP under Rajnath shrugged off bondage to Advani.

An era came to an end and a new one began. Generational shift in leadership unveiled quantum leap in BJP's acceptance in regions where the party had no footprints. The generational shift was dramatic and painful, but renewal of the BJP was the end result. The new leader had stature and ability to raise resources to mount a campaign at a scale that was too high for his rivals. His foes ended dwarfed.

Muddied waters

LIFE begins on a beautiful note, but ends with painful withering.

Manmohan Singh was first from the ranks of Congress with no dynasty lineage to complete two full terms in the office. He shone on the political horizon of India as a star. In latter parts of his career, he was eclipsed by monstrous darkness of scams. He bid adieu to Prime Minister's office in such a manner that he had to beg history for kindness. He withdrew with his personal record blackened beyond redemption. He stayed firm in the office as Prime Minister, but faith of people in Indian institutions was shaken. He was more loyal to 10, Janpath then national interest. Under his watch, India saw anarchy gaining popularity, while loot of the public exchequer reached unimaginable scale.

Singh's debut in politics was nothing short of a beautiful burst of freshness. In PV Narsimha Rao as a mentor, he was bold enough to bring fundamental change to the Indian economy. He was Finance Minister at a time when India faced balance of payment crisis. He put India on the path of economic liberalization. After near four decades of Soviet way of thinking, India admitted the changed realities of the world.

Singh began un-Sovieting India. Under Rao, he was an economist Finance Minister par excellence.

Singh's golden chapters of his personal biography were written when he worked under a seasoned political master in Rao. His forgettable years were when he occupied the top political post of the country and had a boss outside the government. Sonia Gandhi pulled strings often. Singh spent a decade as India's Prime Minister pulled in all directions by disobedient and discordant ministers who were more loyal to their 'Madam' than their Constitutional boss. Prime Minister owed his position not to his political following, but to the largess of Sonia.

He drew strength not from people of the country, but Congress president. Sonia is not a politician in true nature. She is a symbol to which Congressmen submitted. She never held a position of responsibility to have a sense of accountability. Singh was her sacrificial goat. If Singh ever writes his autobiography, he should enlighten his readers with reasons of his compulsions to not quit when he knew his Cabinet consisted of scamsters, who indulged in the loot of the wealth of the nation. Singh belonged to India's economic bureaucracy. He had held several positions before Rao picked him for the post of the Finance Minister. Having been so close to the system, it would be hard to believe that he was not aware of the ways the national exchequer was looted by unscrupulous political class in cahoots with bureaucrats and business class during the decade he was Prime Minister of the country.

He began his stay in the 7, Race Course Road as an honest and learned man. India, incidentally, is a nation where learned men are respected. Singh suited the needs of Sonia the most. Just a few years ago, when faced with political irrelevance amidst the rise of the BJP, Congress had relapsed to the Gandhi dynasty. The Congress was groping for ways to revive. In 2003, as Congress leader Jairam Ramesh would say umpteen times later, 'not even a dog came to 24, Akbar road party headquarters, and it required a lot of persuasions to get leaders to come there to attend meetings'. 'No one gave Congress even a slight chance in the 2004 elections, when Atal Bihari Vajpayee was at the peak of his popularity.'

But the Congress did stage a comeback in 2004 after a gap of eight years. The office of the Prime Minister, however, eluded the Gandhis. No one from the Gandhi family has become Prime Minister since 1989. Sonia's sacrificial feat suited Congress' propaganda machine to connect with the people. She was portrayed as a goddess of sacrifice. Even temples for her sprouted in Andhra Pradesh. But she was still haunted by the acts of Rao and Sitaram Keshri who had sought to free Congress from the influence of the dynasty. She did the next best thing as advised by her coterie. She allowed Congress leaders and Cabinet ministers to become loose cannons against their own government. Singh was Prime Minister without commanding loyalty of party leaders and least of his ministers.

Loyalty disconnect affected his Cabinet. Ministers flaunted their loyalties to 10, Janpath to belittle the office of the Prime Minister. Soon, constituents of the UPA also carved out autonomy in ministries allocated to them. Singh seemed like Mughal king Shah Alam-II. He had brought glorious history of his predecessors to a ridicule. During the reign of Shah Alam-II courtiers and courtesans sold precious royal utensils in open market to maintain their respective lifestyles. Singh was a titular head of UPA for a decade. He scripted sorry tales of political class, bureaucrats, and business houses dipping in national assets for their riches.

In Singh's times, his ministers sparred often. His senior most minister Pranab Mukherjee was allegedly snooped. When P Chidambaram was Minister for Home Affairs he only desired getting the Finance portfolio back. Mukherjee and Chidambaram fought their own battles. Quarrelsome spectacle spilled over in the public domain. Singh at the instance of Sonia had to broker peace between two of his senior most Cabinet colleagues. They sparred and Indian economy went into a tailspin.

Singh's another senior minister and political heavyweight Sharad Pawar sparred with another minister KV Thomas, who had direct access to 10, Janpath. They contradicted each other with remarkable consistency. Aides of Thomas would say that Pawar was Minister of Agriculture to serve interests of various businesses. Pawar would argue for export of onions, sugar, and grains. Thomas would say, 'why export when we have so many people here to serve first'.

Another heavyweight minister Anand Sharma would always be at loggerhead with Jairam Ramesh, who was assigned the task to draft a politically suitable land acquisition bill to boost stock of Rahul Gandhi. Sharma as Minister of Commerce would red-flag Ramesh's ideas on land bill. He would warn that measures proposed would harm India's economy. Mamata Banerjee was Minister of Railways during UPA-I. She stopped attending Cabinet meetings after Mukherjee reportedly snubbed her in such a manner that she was all in tears. Cabinet proposals concerning her ministry would be taken to Kolkata for her vetting.

'No decision is the best decision' became mantra of the UPA government. He took a few decisions lately. They came when his ship had sunk deep in the mid-sea. Investors opted to wait and they waited quite long for change of guard in New Delhi.

The UPA was an alliance consisting of powerful regional parties. Likes of the Left (UPA-I), RJD, Trinamool Congress (UPA-II), DMK, Nationalist Congress Party (NCP), and National Conference were in the alliance. They were in the government with strong numbers under their respective belts. Their leaders had more political experiences than Singh. They were politically strong in their territories, and, hence, did not need to procrastinate at 10, Janpath. They got the wind that Singh was a helpless entity soon enough. They charted their own courses with much disdain. Under the pretext of coalition compulsion, ministers from regional parties acted independently. They swiftly directed advises of Prime Minister to nearest dustbins.

Singh's decade long reign as Prime Minister had four sets of ministers. They were scam masters, no decisions takers, status-quoist, and 'I know all' men. AK Antony was Singh's another key minister. He was Defence Minister. He commanded absolute trust of 10, Janpath. He epitomized Congress in entirety. He believed in 'no decision is best decision' mantra. His inaction is legendary and part of folklore in Congress circles. Tales of his penchant for inaction are aplenty. One day an old man from Kerala landed at his official residence in New Delhi. He wanted a ration card for his family to avail food grains under public distribution system. Antony dismissed him, saying he should meet officials in his district, or the minister concerned in the state. The old man was not in a hurry to act on Antony's advises. He pleaded his case more strongly. An aide of Antony had to intervene to find a solution. The aide told Antony, 'the old man came all the way from Kerala with hopes with a legitimate request. If you do not help him, he will be highly disappointed and share his agony with people back home. You must help him, because he has a lot of hope from you.' An irritated Antony then asked for a letter sent under his name to the concerned minister in Kerala with request to do the needful.

Antony is known for honesty. He is Sonia's man when Congress has to constitute any 'soul-searching' and 'political assessment' exercises. Once he is named to head a committee, immediate crisis in Congress dies down, because leaders know that Antony would give his reports after such time that by then even they would have forgotten what was the issue. Antony's eagerness to stay clean is also legendary. He would dismiss anyone who tries to present him a shawl or a gift. His approach is 'just stay away from such acts'.

In contrast, CPI leader Indrajit Gupta was a Home Minister (1996-98) and renowned for his honesty as well. When he was presented with shawls or other gifts, he would hand over them to the first person he would come across in his office. Jagmohan, who was a minister in

Vajpayee's Cabinet, is also famed for honesty. He would ensure all his gifts, including shawls, are distributed at Sai Mandir on Lodi Road in New Delhi. He never carried any gifts to his home. But Antony's case is a class apart. He carried his habit to the matters of taking decisions on defence procurement. He would not take any decision and would get so many layers made for tenders on procurement that negotiations would continue for years and years. No meaningful defence assets were acquired during Singh's times. Antony would not touch anything for fear of his hands getting dirty.

The UPA-I (2004-09) completed the tenure with round the year 'barking' of the Left parties. After barking, their much threatened 'bite' came when turbaned Prime Minister put his foot down on an issue close to his heart. India and the US had progressed quite significantly on civilian nuclear co-operation, which was an offshoot of the Strobe Talbott-Jaswant Singh parleys in the aftermath of Pokharan nuclear test in 1998. The Left swearing to anti-Americanism withdrew the support. Afterwards New Delhi hosted a drama full of twists and colour. The Left was well aware that all chief ministers of Uttar Pradesh dream of becoming Prime Minister one day. Bahujan Samajwadi Party (BSP) supremo and Dalit queen Mayawati had a year back shone with a stellar electoral performance on the horizon of Indian politics. After a decade, her party was the first to get an absolute majority in Uttar Pradesh. She had scripted a social engineering, which had become a case study for other political parties.

Gurudwara Raqabganj Road in New Delhi hosts a trust in the name of BSP founder Kanshi Ram and adjacent to it is party headquarters. Both the buildings are inter-connected. If one takes a tour of the building assets, he would not avoid being wonder struck. Party headquarters of Congress and BJP would appear extremely poor siblings. Even the best of the five-star hotels in New Delhi would not have facilities of Mayawati's building assets right in the heart of the national capital. The Left and Mayawati would hold parleys there to search for a strategy to bring down Singh's government. The Left made her believe that she could be Prime Minister of the country. And intoxicated with the dreams sold to her by Prakash Karat and Sitaram Yechury, Mayawati then set on the course to get numbers in Lok Sabha to her side and topple Singh's government. Afterwards, members of Parliament would tell, that astronomical figures were being offered to them to switch sides.

Little away an equally dramatic day after day spectacle went on at 27, Lodhi Estate. The address was not as awe inspiring as Mayawati's abode, but had all facilities for which a rich man goes to a five star hotel. It was the residence of Amar Singh. He was the man Friday of Samajwadi Party chief Mulayam Singh Yadav. He plotted counter moves against Mayawati for upcoming vote of trust in Lok Sabha on the issue of Indo-US nuclear deal (2008). Singh would often call up Amar Singh to enlist his support to bail out his government. Left counted on Yadav. They were ideological neighbours. Marxism and socialism have worked together in India for decades. Left was not aware that Yadav had no passion to keep his words. Yadav and Amar Singh outsmarted Mayawati and her Left strategists to save Singh's government. Though the UPA survived to live another day, 'dirty tricks' employed to gain confidence in Lok Sabha became talk of the town.

India would subsequently be hit by an avalanche of scams. India's top auditor -- Comptroller and Auditor General -- under Vinod Rai would reveal losses to national exchequer, all notional, of unheard amounts. They were caused by dubious ways adopted by the government to allocate 2G spectrum and coal-blocks. Scams related to Commonwealth Games, Adarsh Housing Society and some others took the form of quite a lavish bouquet of corruptions committed right under the nose of Singh.

Singh as Finance Minister had begun taking steps to un-Soviet India. In an ironical twist, he signed off his career as Prime Minister giving his nod to moves which were essentially obsolete Soviet ways. Pawar had warned that the National Food Security Bill if enacted by Parliament would make India another Soviet Russia. The Bill sought to cover 75 per cent of rural population and 50 per cent in urban areas for highly subsidized food grains entitlements programme. The estimated cost to roll out the scheme was about $25 billion a year to begin with. Singh with a lot of reluctance agreed to clear the Bill in the Cabinet, after Sonia made it a prestige issue. Once after a Cabinet meeting postponed a decision on the Food Bill, Thomas, minister who drafted the legislative proposal, is said to have gone straight to 10, Janpath from 7, Race Course Road and cried his heart out at 'ways of a few ministers to scuttle revolutionary plan'. He complained of attempts of sabotage from within the ranks of the Singh's Cabinet. Sonia was moved and angered. She did not waste much of time to dial Singh to demand to know why and who were sabotaging the Bill. A pliant Singh ensured it was cleared in the next Cabinet meeting.

Even after two years of the enactment of the National Food Security Act by Parliament, the 'revolutionary' plan lives on the paper. This piece of legislative proposal was given in a 'ready-made' form by National Advisory Council headed by Sonia. This body consisted of NGO activists and retired bureaucrats. The law is full of such bureaucratic maze, which needs to be in place before it's rolled out, that the possibility of a silent death is not entirely ruled out.

The UPA-II (2009-14) was held captive by tentacles of NGOs, which spread in all the ministries and commanded enough power to paralyze the governance itself. Sonia's son -- Rahul Gandhi -- was in-charge of the Youth Congress and National Students Union of India (NSUI) for larger parts of the Singh era. Sons and daughters of the elite India studying abroad sensed opportunity to exploit Rahul's disconnect with the mass. They joined the Youth Congress in big numbers when Rahul looked for talents outside the Congress cadre, which for him meant an educational degree from the US or the UK. But that would not be the end of the story. Picking up the Rahul thread this elite class snaked into various ministries and ensured plumb posts to call shots in the affairs of the government.

Flaunting their reach to Rahul, they were most sought after by the ministers. Muhammed Khan was one such blue-eyed Rahul 'discovered' talent in the Ministry of Rural Development tagged to Ramesh who drafted such a tricky and bureaucratic land acquisition law that India is not yet out of knots into which the law bound it. This elite crop perched at key positions in the Singh government planted ideas in the mind of Rahul largely influenced by Left leaning NGOs and subsequently got the ministries to act accordingly. They short-circuited top echelons of bureaucracy. Their offices would keep doors open for activists from NGOs.

Bureaucracy first stopped working. Later, they began making distance. These elite young 'politicians' would show off that they read Hindi newspapers and would try speaking in Hindi to give a semblance of being connected with grounds. Some of them would solicit the company of Hindi newspaper journalists to get the words correct and letters drafted in common spoken language. Senior Congress leaders would lament that those 'who never saw a village in their lives are eyes and ears of Rahul'.

Rahul had showcased a Youth Congress convention on the outskirts of Delhi as 'Buniyaad' (2011) to which all Ministers, including Prime Minister, had made a beeline to attend. Though it was for talents nursed by Rahul in Youth Congress to brainstorm, the platform rather emerged as indoctrination of the young leaders at the hands of the ultra-Left leaning NGO leaders. By then Rahul had metamorphosed as an ultra-Leftist leader, who would appear at any place to ensure that no land was acquired for the industries. His brigade of elite young 'politicians' would romanticize works of NGOs against the industries and would soon prevail over the Minister for environment to emerge as a terror agency for those who sought to establish industrial houses. Odisha will bear the brunt in big ways for Rahul's brand of politics.

Singh watched helplessly, as Rahul switched off engine of his government and handed over keys to NGOs. It would be these people who would draft the 'Land Acquisition and Resettlement and Rehabilitation Bill, 2011' later named 'The Right to Fair Compensation and Transparency in Land Acquisition, Rehabilitation and Resettlement Act, 2013'. The National Highways Authority of India (NHAI) in a 'white paper' unofficially circulated to media after Modi government assumed office would accuse this law for having brought road constructions to a grinding halt, as none wanted to part with their land and acquiring land became 'near impossible'.

Sonia and Rahul with their penchant for wisdom sourced from NGOs derailed India's growth. Even a five per cent GDP growth was a challenge for Singh. Sonia had robbed Singh of power in manners not seen by people. Rahul went a step further and ridiculed Prime Minister at a time when he was in the US on an important bilateral trip by barging into a presser being held by Ajay Maken at Indian Press Club on Raisina Road by telling that a Cabinet approved proposal (2013) to shield political leaders caught in court cases was worth tearing apart and throwing into a dustbin.

Singh would not think of quitting even when he was robbed off all the honours. In place, he would counsel Rahul. His weakness to stay with the chair would cost India a great deal, as hopelessness and cynicism became norms. Buffoons in Congress had converted Singh to their clan. Singh pleaded history to be kinder to him than contemporary media. Contemporary history has no parallel to understand how and why Singh allowed Congress to derail India. The least that he could have done was to have quit when he was not heard by his ministers. If he had done so, history may have glorified him.

In his times civil society laid siege to New Delhi. Television lived off mobs brought in at Jantar Mantar by the civil society. They would shake up Singh government in a manner that it would further drown into policy paralysis. An avalanche of negativism struck India.

Lion & Fox

INDIA is a fertile land of event management.

People have natural talents to become crowd. Snake charmers and herb sellers from mountains knowing remedies for ailments of all kinds have gathered crowds for ages at ease in India. They have inspired others and their art is now no more exclusive to them.

One morning a fragile looking man in loose trouser and untucked full-sleeve shirt wearing unpolished sandals gathered a few journalists around him on Jantar Mantar. He pleaded for media support. 'If you support us, we can make it big.' Television journalists offered fulsome support and offered suggestions on ways to gather more people to give a semblance of a movement in the making. The man lapped advises and profusely thanked them.

He was Arvind Kejriwal. He then headed an NGO called 'Public Cause and Research Foundation (PCRF)'. He also had another NGPO called 'Parivartan'. On that morning his event was staged at Jantar Mantar, with Maharashtrian expert in 'fast unto death' agitations – Kisan Baburao 'Anna' Hazare -- in principal role. Two had come together for Jan Lokpal, an Ombudsman Law.

Even before Anna Hazare joined him, Kejriwal had led many marches on Jantar Mantar for Jan Lokpal. But none paid attention, including footage hungry television media. He would lead motley of former bureaucrats and NGO activists at Jantar Mantar for Jan Lokpal. Their marches did not make to even the inside pages of newspapers. India had not yet known that the country was scam ridden. Kejriwal had to wait a little more to attract the media attention. The Commonwealth Games 2010 hosted in Delhi turned the public sentiment for Congress and UPA sour after spate of corruption cases surfaced. Soon scams after scams hit the headlines and Kejriwal discovered that the media had begun taking interest in him.

Hazare had successfully led some agitations in Maharashtra. He was part of campaign for Right to Information. He had fame. He lived in a temple in his village. He was seen as a credible face. On April 5, 2011 when summer had not yet taken Delhi in its arms in full might, Hazare began his 'fast unto death'.

Kejriwal had quit Indian Revenue Services to launch an NGO, which worked for the multi-holes afflicted public distribution system (PDS) through which the government channeled over $15 billion each year for food subsidy. The PDS is a moth-eaten system. Various government agencies have pegged leakages to the extent of 50 per cent. He was also with bureaucrat turned activist Aruna Roy in the campaign for Right to Information. Activists in civil society space had known that their clouts were on the rise and a government mired in scams was most vulnerable to their sustained campaigns.

The RSS runs an educational institution called 'Sankalp' where students get almost free hostel and coaching facilities for examinations conducted by Union Public Service Commission (UPSC) for All India Services such as IAS, IPS, etc. The RSS is not alone in doing so, for Hamdard University in outer Delhi also has similar arrangement on much large scales for Muslims. Those who had taken facilities of 'Sankalp' in late 1990s recall Kejriwal teaching economics and current affairs.

Kodipakam Neelameghacharya Govindacharya was an influential RSS pracharak (bachelor worker). He became power centre in BJP when Advani was at the peak of his career. Renowned within BJP and outside for his intellectual sharpness and ability to write with both hands at the same time on different subjects, Govindacharya evolved as top ideologue of the BJP. He was brain behind Advani embarking on the path of 'Hindutva' and 'Ramjanmbhoomi' campaign. In his days of glory, he committed a mistake. He had spoken a truth. He said, it was not

Vajpayee, who was the Prime Minister then, but Advani, deputy Prime Minister, who called shots in the government. He called Vajpayee a 'mukhouta (mask)' in the same breath. Among all attributes, discipline in RSS is sacrosanct and non-negotiable. The wrath of a furious Vajpayee fell on Govindacharya. Advani had to sacrifice him. He was banished from the BJP.

Later, he emerged staunch critic of both the Congress and the BJP. He advocates an alternative political system wherein citizens take leading roles. He does not favour any established political parties. Govindacharya saw hope and possibility of his ideas transforming into reality through Kejriwal. The former saffronite was an organizational man of unmatched caliber. Many pracharaks and RSS functionaries, who were disillusioned with the BJP imbibing vices of the Congress, stayed in touch with Govindacharya. They still see hopes in him. Jantar Mantar and later Ramlila Ground would become the stage for bonding of Govindacharya and Arvind Kejriwal without being seen by the people. Former BJP ideologue never came in the open and always stayed behind the doors. He played his part as a strategist.

Much before Kejriwal hit headlines, he would generously employ journalists at the Kaushambi office of his NGO. Doors for journalists will always remain open at Parivartan. Much before he would need help of press to magnify his campaign for Jan Lokpal, Kejriwal had co-opted the media. Television had given recognition to a few of journalists. Their sense of importance was disproportionate to their achievements. Their minds had spun and thought more as activists than journalists. They found in Kejriwal a perfect carrier of their frustration with the 'system'. Professional lines blurred. But no fingers were raised. Kejriwal was able to count on many journalists. They would freely advise him on how to build his campaign. Journalists would also tip off Kejriwal about the impending moves of the government to tackle his agitation. These journalists acted as spies for Kejriwal when ministers of Manmohan Singh government freely shared strategies to deal with civil society agitations. Kejriwal ensured his journalist friends to stay in their professions with an open offer to join him if he made it big. kejriwal did make it big subsequently and he embraced a few of the journalists who were placed in his core team. Some other journalist friends of Kejriwal are still in the profession to serve his interests. When Hazare began his 'fast unto death', a television journalist too joined him. A professional media house should have sacked him, but he emerged a toast.

Kejriwal was inspired by Arab Spring and people's revolution at Tahrir Square (2011). He thought India too could host events taking place in West Asia and Africa. With Hazare on stage, Kejriwal would make it a point to mention Tahrir Square umpteen times, while speaking to motley of television crews present at Jantar Mantar. He would, however, be clever enough to state that Jantar Mantar is not a Tahrir Square.

Jawaharlal Nehru University spread over 1,000 acres in South Delhi has an umbilical cord with Jantar Mantar. Students turned activists of this university are more than eager to become a mob for any agitation against government of the day at Jantar Mantar. They solved woes of Arvind Kejriwal on how to build crowd and sustain them for whole day to enthuse television crews. He sought to give Hazare a makeover. Maharashtrian agitator would speak his mind about democracy for a while, which would not be understood by most in the audience. Kejriwal and his rabble rouser colleagues would run down political class. For them, the whole political class consisted of thieves. With musical band on stage and theater artists on road, Kejriwal had woven a good script for a political event with entertainment to keep television crews busy.

By the time Kejriwal staged his Jan Lokpal event at Jantar Mantar, India had seen two decades of judicial activism. Lawyers had made good use of Public Interest Litigation (PIL) to become celebrities. Like television anchors, these lawyers too thought that they deserved to play a larger role in public space. They would bombard governments of the day with PILs. Half of bureaucrats of Delhi government would be appearing before Delhi High Court or Supreme Court on a daily basis after being dragged in plethora of cases filed against various departments. From education to health, from pollution to traffic management, from distribution of food grains to fixing electricity tariff, judiciary was issuing direction to government on a regular basis.

Judiciary was seen encroaching into the territory marked for executive. Many lawyers specialized in PILs. Prashant Bhushan was on top of that class. He is son of lawyer-turned-politician Shanti Bhushan, who was once Law Minister. Shanti Bhushan in those days would proudly tell that he dedicated his son Prashant Bhushan for national cause, while his other sons made money in the lucrative profession of law. Shanti Bhushan would give inaugural donation of 10 million rupees when Aam Admi Party was founded at Constitution Club near Indian Parliament. He along with his son was instrumental in drafting of Jan Lokpal Bill. His son ensured through a volley of PILs in Supreme Court that the Manmohan Singh government had egg on its face repeatedly.

With Kejriwal on his side, Prashant Bhushan would spew venom against the UPA government. Together, they would strip the UPA government and Congress naked in a span of a few months in 2011. Prashant Bhushan is ideologically a Leftist. But he's different from the mainstream Leftists in the sense that his ideas are more rabid. He believes that Indian democracy is a sham, because it's 'minimal' in scope with electorates casting their votes once in five years and have no more role in functioning of a government. He vouches for referendum in Kashmir, and is against deployment of security forces against Maoist extremists.

Prashant Bhushan fortified Kejriwal against any legal ramifications even though he hurled allegations at Union Ministers and politicians in a manner as if he had been stricken by verbal diarrhea. Pashant Bhushan provided Kejriwal a license to run down political class with impunity. Kejriwal had such candour, that he would name half the Manmohan Singh Cabinet ministers as corrupt with claims that they should have been in jail if there had been a Lokpal. He would give his verdict in clear kangaroo court style at Janatar Mantar. He would be egged on by a 'lynch' mob consisting of a few hundreds. His evidences for 'corrupt-branding' would be newspaper reports.

When Hazare sat on fast unto death' at Jantar Mantar in April, 2011, the UPA was already handicapped by judicial activism along with widespread agitations spearheaded by civil society. In a span of just four days of 'fast unto death', the government wilted and gave in. It agreed to Kejriwal's demand for a joint drafting committee of Lokpal Bill, consisting of half the members from the government and rest from his Jantar Mantar brigade. He had drawn his pound of flesh from a government, which had lost its moral halo.

Afterwards kejriwal never had to look back. His profile grew exponentially. Soon he was bigger than Hazare. He conveniently charted an independent course. Kejriwal's tactics was outright blackmailing of the government over consequences of 'fast unto death' of the Maharashtrian activist. He used Hazare as his weapon to further his interests. Hazare is a person with questionable ability to understand intricacies of law making. He was not aware of the fact, that Kejriwal was building his profile on the pretext of Jan Lokpal campaign for his eventual plunge into politics. New Delhi thugs had taken Hazare for a ride.

During 13 days long fast by the Gandhian activist at Ramlila Ground where the RSS workers swelled the crowd, Hazare looked a helpless men. Kejriwal pushed him on an extended 'fast unto death'. The Maharashtrian leader realized that Kejriwal was playing with his life. Each day Kejriwal would tell television crews that if any untoward thing happened to Hazare, the blame would lie with the government. Vilas Rao Deshmukh understood the pain of Hazare. He arranged for a Marathi mediator and the stir was called off. The government gave token promises to Hazare. The Maharashtrian called off his fast unto death on August 28, 2011. Hazare and Kejriwal knew at Ramlila Ground, that they had to go separate ways. Kejriwal began feeding media that Hazare had been managed by the Congress.

Much water had flown into the Ganges by then. The Congress was struck by a typhoon of allegations. Kejriwal would return to Jantar Mantar to tell his lynch mob that if there was Jan Lokpal in place not less than 25 ministers of the Manmohan Singh Cabinet would have been in jail. Lokpal was passed by Parliament in 2013. No minister of Manmohan Singh Cabinet has yet gone to the jail. The Lokpal has not been constituted even. And no one is crying anymore on Jantar Mantar Road why the Modi government is not putting in place a Lokpal. Even the Kejriwal led Delhi government has constituted Lokayukta as envisaged in the law. There is no Lokayukta in Delhi as of now. No one wants Lokpal anymore. The characters has come on Jantar Mantar not for Lokpal, but for power and they have achieved their objectives. So, convenient silence prevails over.

Emboldened by Jan Lokpal campaign, Baba Ramdev, originally Ramkrishne Yadav, too rushed to New Delhi for an indefinite fast. He wanted government to bring back black money stashed in tax havens in a matter of a few days. When he landed at New Delhi airport, Cabinet ministers – Pranab Mukherjee, Kapil Sibal, Pawan Kumar Bansal, and Subodh Kant Sahay – all were there to receive and cajole him not to go ahead with his agitation. One senior minister had different opinion than those who had laid out red-carpet welcome to Yoga Guru. He was Polaniappan Chidambaram. He was Minister for Home Affairs with control over Delhi police. On June 2, 2011, Baba Ramdev kept government on its toes and was far from being persuaded by promises of actions against black money. P Chidambaram kept himself away. Sensing trouble in the making, Sibal had long telephonic interactions with Chidambaram on that evening during which he pleaded to 'engage the Baba'. Chidambaram was not persuaded. He wanted to show that some spine was still left in the government. On the midnight of June 5, Ramdev and his followers faced the full might of Delhi police. Ramdev ran away wearing a woman's clothes. The agitation was crushed. Ramdev never again tried to take on the government. He went to Gandhinagar where he surrendered to Narendra Modi.

Jan Lokpal campaign delivered serious blow to Congress base in Delhi. After 15 years of being in power in Delhi, chief minister Sheila Dikshit was handed over humiliating defeat in 2013 Assembly elections. She had no choice but to retire from active politics. A year after all Congress MPs in Delhi would meet the similar fate. The Congress was finished in the national capital. Politics is an art of managing perceptions. The Congress had no answer to its image muddied in public after Jantar Mantar and Ramlila ground agitations. It left government to fend for itself. The gust of anger fanned by Hazare and Kejriwal would soon spread length and breadth of the country. With television media in lynch' mode,

Kejriwal-Bhushan combination would fill the air with intense negativism.

They believed in the writings of Pierre-Joseph Proudhan, a French and first self-proclaimed anarchist, who published 'What is property' in 1840 wherein he propounded the idea of anarchism. He gave the theory of 'spontaneous order'. He believed that organization would emerge through peaceful evolution imposing its own idea of order without a central coordinator against the wills of individuals. His idea was that people have capacity to throw an alternative to existing system. Vacuum was unnatural. When Kejriwal would be asked on allegations against him of spreading too much of negativity without offering a platform to channel people's anger, he would say 'people will spontaneously throw an alternative'.

Future course of events proved that Kejriwal was partially correct in reading political trajectory of India. Delhi has a population of about 20 million. Kejriwal's party became an alternative and filled the vacuum in the capital city. India would, however, prove to be too large for Kejriwal. India would seek not just an angry man who could fuel public anger, but someone who could scale up ambitions of people and seen capable to deliver on them.

Kejriwal-Bhushan duo had just prepared grounds for Modi to launch a unique election campaign at such a scale that all his rivals would be dwarfed. He seized the opportunity thrown to him by both hands. His electoral kite flew higher and higher with the winds of negativism flowing intensely. He found people receptive to each word that he uttered. He offered dreams at scales not imagined by people. Kejriwal was king of negativism. But his kingdom did not spread beyond the capital city of Delhi. India was not yet a fertile land for anarchism. Kejriwal's anarchism was space bound. He sowed seeds. Modi harvested the bumper crops.

Changelessness

POLITICAL power grows out of the barrel of a gun was a prophetic maxim of Mao Zedong made in 1927.

Even after about nine decades, China stay bound by the slogan. India is China's immediate neighbor with similar civilization. Yet, India charted a different course. India, though, is not a country of guns or militia. India chose ballot to bullet. But after the demise of Pandit Jawahar Lal Nehru, political evolution saw Zedong's prescription practiced by political outfits in little revised form. And, thus, the slogan metamorphosed into 'political power grows out of empty stomach of poor'.

In the death of Nehru, India did not lose only a great statesman. Followed by sudden death of Lal Bahadur Shastri in close heels, curtain came down on India's finest breed of political leaders. Indian freedom struggle had nourished in its bosom spotless and selfless political leadership. The fire of independence movement burnt in the belly of leaders to join them in the selfless service of nation building. The blessed breed arguably lasted till the times of Shastri. After his death, the institution of selfless politics devoted to nation building began withering.

The era of self-interest driven slugfest to carve out political territories began with maddening burst. But Nehru's death and not that of Shastri should mark turning point in political history of India. Though Shastri showed sparks of brilliance in his short stint at the top, he led the country too briefly to change the course of the country or drop too deep an anchor. The void after Shastri's untimely death revealed epochal political leadership vacuum. Nehru's reign was too long to allow emergence of a statesmen of his kind. His successors lacked stature to capture imagination of the people. They failed to understand need of the nation. The poverty of leadership gave ways to slugfest among surviving political class to carve out their respective territories on narrow considerations.

Leaders, who had played major roles in India attaining her freedom from several centuries of slavery, had led people by examples. They lived selfless lives. They left behind legendary tales of honesty and probity in their public and personal lives. National Archives is a living testimony of the high standard with which the first generation of political leaders, who spent their youth battling the British, led the nation. India's misfortune was that such leaders did not live long enough past the freedom of the country. They were honest, because they were selfless. After they departed, India lost the breed of selfless political leaders. Corruption is a byproduct of self-centered politics. The nation and people ceased to be priorities of leaders who sought to fill the void left by India's first generation of leaders.

All great men have their own share of frailties; else they may have been Gods.

Nehru committed a great disservice to the nation by planting seeds of a political dynasty. He nurtured his daughter Indira Gandhi for political roles. It would be quite naive to entertain the idea that Nehru did not foresee a political dynasty taking roots in his name. It would be equally naive to believe that he allowed democratic spirits within the Congress to take deep roots to stall a dynasty in his name. He arguably knew India better than anyone in his times, and history must record his failure.

British had turned India into a consumer of industrial world. And Nehru sought to reverse the trend and lay grounds for robust industrialization. He tied up with foreign industrial leaders and a few large manufacturing units took roots. He partnered with foreign countries to incubate Indian Institute of Technology (IITs). In his reign, he kept the window open to get the best of the world. His modern temples (large factories) became giants in later years. But his demise shut the doors on industrial expansion. In subsequent decades following his death, India became a nation of scarcity. Such a situation suited political masters of the country. Irony was that the daughter subverted her father's blueprint to make India an industrially strong-footed country. Nehru was an internationalist. His daughter was an opposite who shut India's doors on the world.

India arguably disowned Nehru after China bruised national pride in the 1962 war. Subsequently, Nehru's blueprint to herald renaissance in the economy found no takers among his successors. Nehru sought to crush the Left during his times, but his daughter embraced their ideology in her statecraft.

Indira seeded the idea of povertarian politics. In the next one and a half decades she institutionalized the politics of povertarianism. As a byproduct, corruption spread its tentacles as the politics of povertarianism unveiled the Soviet ways of statecraft. State agencies owned everything. The scarcity of all kinds hit the people in all its might. The state agencies birthed a class, which continue to pocket almost half the state wealth transferred to the people through various means. The cancer of corruption not only got institutionalized because of the Soviet ways of governance, but also took form of a culture. With employments nowhere to be found except in the government wings, the natural choice was to seek parasitical roles in agencies transferring state wealth to the people. The Congress too forgot greatest icon of the party in Nehru and embraced Indira and her ways religiously. The religiosity in ways of politics of the Congress birthed the widespread and institutionalized form of sycophancy for the first family. Thus, povertarianism, corruption and sycophancy were all interwoven in such harmony not to be found anywhere.

Indira was an empress of artificial scarcity of goods and services. Citizens resorted to bribe those with access to state agencies to fulfil their wants. If not for the liberation of Bangladesh and India handing out crushing defeat to Pakistan in 1971 war, history may have been very unkind to Indira. Her forte surely was clarity of the mind unlike some of her predecessors, who sought legitimacy for their actions from international powers. She cared the least for such internationalism and that helped her to help the people outgrow the 1962 humiliation.

The Congress under her stewardship invented slogan of 'India is Indira; Indira is India' to institutionalize terminal disease of sycophancy. The disease took the shape of a monster during the times of Rajiv Gandhi. Under Sonia, it became larger than the party. With the Congress losing connect with the people in subsequent decades, this terminal disease turned fatal for the party and also for the nation.

The Congress is now being led by the fifth generation of leadership for all practical purposes by Rahul Gandhi. In actions, he has shown to be the Greek God of sycophancy. The Congress is not just a political party, but a culture where the art of survival is perfected in the guise of dynasty worship. What is Congress? It's answered by a joke heard at party headquarter -- 24, Akbar Road, New Delhi. Two Congress men locked in fist-fights when they see Sonia appearing in their sight stop their duel and immediately wear broad smiles to raise the cry at the top of their lung: 'Sonia Gandhi zindabad'.

With the Congress enjoying monopoly over the politics of poverty and also strong support base in rural India till the demise of Indira, its opponents sheltered behind the idea of socialism. They perfected the art of politics of caste subsequently. Socialist politics in India had not much of an organizational support base. They flickered on the political horizon in the form of a few stars -- Jayaprakash Narain (JP), Ram Manohar Lohiya, and Karpoori Thakur -- and faded away quickly. But they did leave behind trails of caste chieftains, who claimed legacy of JP and Ram Manohar Lohiya. They carved out territories to birth family controlled political enterprises. Haryana, Uttar Pradesh, and Bihar proved fertile grounds for them. The likes of Devi Lal, Mulayam Singh Yadav, and Lalu Prasad raised their political outfits in Haryana, Uttar Pradesh and Bihar where one particular caste was numerically dominant.

India witnessed regular burst of Janata experiments. But the outcome was such that people became wary of trusting them with power at the national level. Yet, they succeeded in becoming strong provincial leaders. Viswanath Pratap Singh popped up in late 1980s as a political fidayeen to destroy Rajiv. He was instrumental in making people believe not only in urban centers but also in rural areas, that the Congress and corruption were two sides of the same coin. 'Yeh jo gaal ki laali hai, yeh Bofors ki dalaali hai (The rosy cheeks are due to kickbacks of Bofors)' was the slogan which struck popular chord in most parts of North, East and Central India in the 1989 elections. The slogan obviously was for Rajiv.

Janata Dal, which VP Singh led as the Congress rebel turned socialist, was essentially a loose confederation of a few egoist regional satraps whose ambitions were disproportionate to their respective support bases. The Janata Party fiasco of 1970s repeated in the collapse of Janata Dal in 1990s. But it was not before VP Singh brought caste into the forefront of Indian politics by implementing the Mandal Commission report for caste based reservations in jobs and educational institutions. The BJP sought to counter further fragmentation of 'Hindu' vote base on caste lines by embracing religion in full force in its bid to expand beyond few pockets in North India.

Lal Krishna Advani gave BJP wings to fly. His campaign for a grand temple for Lord Ram at Ayodhya struck emotional chord with the people. 'Mandir wahin banaayenge...' ranted the air as Advani's Rath (chariot) chugged along from Somnath in Gujrat bound for Ayodhya in Uttar Prdaesh. The Rath was brought to a grinding halt at Sitamarhi in Bihar. The Rath stopped, but the BJP was unstoppable.

Indian political history will remain incomplete if the monumental role of Advani in turning Indian politics on its head is not recorded. He changed the discourse of Indian politics. He exposed the fault lines in Indian politics. 'Pseudo-secularism' became the buzz word. He substantially blunted VP Singh's gameplan to turn other backward castes into one solid political constituency.

Before Advani, none touched raw nerves of the political idea of secularism, which was essentially a ploy to herd Muslims into political slavery. Rajiv's brazenness in overturning Supreme Court decision on Shah Bano issue and his subsequent move to unlock Babri mosque gave Advani an explosive plot to run his surgical knife through the tired and fatigued Congress. The BJP fed with Advani tonic embarked on an exponential rise in the Hindi heartland, besides making substantial inroads in the western India. His toils later helped Vajpayee become Prime Minister. His irony was that he always stayed in the shadow of Vajpayee. But it was to the credit of Advani that the BJP emerged a credible alternative to Congress on the national scene. And for a while people believed that India finally had discovered its two party system, with a few fringe players.

The near monopoly of the Congress in Indian politics ended by 1989. There were more players around and they sliced their shares out of the pie exclusively enjoyed by the Congress till Rajiv frittered away landslide mandate that he had won in 1984. The Congress has since been on steep decline. The tragic assassination of Rajiv pushed the Gandhi dynasty in political oblivion for a few years.

The opportunity was seized by PV Narsimha Rao to combine with Manomohan Singh (1991-96) to begin a new bold exercise to unfetter Indian economy. They were faced with the crisis of India going bankrupt, as the balance of payment situation went haywire. They turned the crisis into an opportunity to unveil the 'big bang' in Indian economy. In doing so, they sought to undo damages done to the Indian economy by decades of inwardness. They opened up the economy and charted the course to clip the wings of 'Inspector Raj'. They forced open the shut windows to the world. And, thus, they infused fresh air into the Indian economy.

The latent talent in India lapped the opportunity by both the hands. India shined on the world map with its talents in electronics and software. Rao unveiled strategic 'Look East' policy, which paid rich dividends later, besides giving India a strategic depth closer to the shores of China. After a few years of political instability, the Vajpayee era set in and he sought to take off from where Rao had left. India saw a decade of consistent efforts to unsoviet the country and shun the inwardness. Vajpayee took the notion of 'big bang' quite seriously and went on to test nuclear explosion at Pokhran in 1998. His sheer audacity in doing so forced the shut doors for India ajar on the world scene. He challenged India's isolation in the big league of the world.

None came forward to give India its due place, but Vajapyee put his feet in the doors which were shut for the country. India withstood knee-jerk reactions of the world. But subsequently Vajpayee's sherpa Jaswant Singh and his US counterpart Strob Talbott laid foundation for much closer Indo-US relations. India's nuclear isolation ended. The world later made a beeline to become part of India's bid to tap nuclear energy. Vajpayee spearheaded India's networking revolution in roads and telecommunication. Roads helped rural India to shrug off reclusive veil. People in rural areas tapped opportunities in urban centres. He also scripted another path-breaking reform through Electricity Act, 2003, which reincarnated moth eaten state electricity boards subsequently. Until the reforms came, none wanted to put even a single penny in the power sector, but in another decade billions of dollars have been poured and it's still counting.

Vajpayee had good reasons to believe that the people would re-elect him in 2004. But New Delhi caucus within the BJP was unaware of realities in the vast country, which had not yet reaped benefits of measures of the NDA government (1998-2004), which were essentially long term in nature. The New Delhi caucus within the BJP embarked on a ludicrous 'India Shining' campaign. It was in contrast to multitude of islands of darkness into which large parts of India slipped into after sunset. They misguided Vajpayee and the tired statesman already on the wrong side of the age had no stomach to see for himself how much of India had actually been shining.

Electoral politics demands tangible outcomes in short spans. Vast majority of the BJP workers thought that the New Delhi caucus within the party deserved a lesson. They did not connect with the people and Vajpayee looked too tired to re-ignite people's faith in him.

None believed in 2004 that the Congress could turn its political fortunes for better. The party office would wear deserted looks in the run up to the 2004 elections. Yet, Congress staged an unprecedented comeback. Sonia proved that the Gandhi dynasty was the only hope for the Congress. Until then the Congress had been out of power for eight years in a row. She shed her reluctance and made a grand entry into Indian politics. She successfully slipped into the shadow of Indira. India was least bothered of her foreign pedigree. She demonstrated that the Congress had deep roots in rural India. The poor of the country looked upon Congress for deliverance when BJP hit the campaign trails wearing the robe of arrogance.

But Sonia found to her dismay that she could not move into 7, Race Course Road. She did not want another Rao as Prime Minister. The choice fell on Manmohan Singh. The Congress showcased her as goddess of sacrifice. Sycophancy further deepened and seeds of disharmony were sown in the functioning of the new government led by United Progressive Alliance (2004-14). Her absolute command over the loyalty of ministers in the UPA gave telling blows to the might of Prime Minister's Office (PMO). Emergence of an extra-Constitutional power center in the form of National Advisory Council (NAC) under her further belittled the PMO. The Maharashtra model of Shiv Sena when Balasaheb Bal Thackeray remote-controlled the government seemed at plays at the national level. However, a formidable combination of better economic conditions and clean image of Manmohan Singh gave the Congress another electoral victory in 2009.

During UPA-I (2004-09) the Congress co-opted the Left in running the government. The Left pulled the Congress ideologically more towards itself in those tumultuous five years. The Left was at its peak strength. It gave a moral anchor to the UPA only to get mortal blows in West Bengal politics for having entered into an alliance with the Congress, which in turn robbed the Soviet-China inspired gang to cede space to the temperamental street fighter Mamata Banerjee. While Karat & Yechury Co were busy in 'barking and biting' the UPA-I, Banerjee had dipped her sharp nails too deep in the political soil of West Bengal to not only uproot the Left, but to throw them into the Bay of Bengal after 34 long years of unchallenged rule.

In UPA-II, the NAC evolved as guiding soul of the government. The NAC was actually a platform hijacked by Non-Governmental Organizations (NGOs) and retired bureaucrats. The NGOs in India have largely acted as facades for vested interests. Bureaucrats obsessed with New Delhi for their post-retirement stay because of better healthcare facilities and access to those clubs where they enjoy their passions find in the NGOs extension of their working life. The NGOs and bureaucrats incidentally are siblings, because the latter nurse the former in the form of investment for their post-retirement benefits. The NAC became a perfect platform for them to serve their vested interests. Soon, the NAC began nibbling the government. The governance took back-seat, and the NGO activism came of age. The NGOs pinned down the government. And, the status quo nature of the Congress and the government became much evident, giving birth to years of policy paralysis.

The government officially stated in 2012 that 21.9 per cent of its population was still below the poverty line. For the government, those with Rs 26 a day in rural areas and Rs 32 in urban centers were poor. The line is drawn at an artificially low level and actually corresponds to the amount that the government can afford for anti-poverty measures. If there is more money with the government, the poverty deciding line could correspondingly go further up.

It would arguably be a human miracle to survive at Rs 26 in villages and Rs 32 in towns. But if a reality-adjusted poverty line is drawn more than one-third of India's population could turn out to be easily poor. This is despite the fact that India embarked on the path of poverty alleviation with the advent of Indira at the helms of affairs. About four and a half decades have gone by since the Congress led by Indira imbibed the idea of practicing the art of 'politics of poverty'. But the poor are yet to see better days.

In contrast, East and South-east Asian countries were able to reduce absolute number of poor by two-third in the last three decades. They could achieve the success on the back of their Gross Domestic Growth (GDP) growing between seven to 10 per cent a year. Rao (1991-96) and Vajpayee (1998-2004) sought to replicate economic successes of East and South-East Asian countries and were successful to some extent but not enough in short time.

A decade of UPA rule brought a pause to expansion of Indian economy at a scale necessary for reducing number of poor. The economy contracted later and so did the government spending for areas, which give leg up to economic activities. The railways did not add additional tracks to clear congestion to carry more passengers and freight. But railways did accumulate projects announced by government through Budgets, which awaited fund allocations to see light of the day. The funds never came. Road constructions came to a grinding halt. By the time the UPA was eased out of power, private companies engaged in road constructions had gone broke. The UPA awarded end number of ultra-mega power projects (UMPP) to private and public enterprises. They endlessly awaited coal-linkages, while state governments moved at snail's pace to get land for them. With infrastructure sector burning balance-sheets of companies, private investments dried up. The spillover effect would soon submerge whole business sentiment. Taint of the 'policy paralysis' would soon stick with the UPA.

Despite no economic expansion under its belt as seen under Rao and Vajpayee, the Congress won the 2009 Lok Sabha elections. Political pundits agreed that the UPA-I could win the elections, because of Mahatma Gandhi National Rural Employment Guarantee Act (MGNREGA), waiver of the farmers' loans (2008), and implementation of the sixth pay commission, which significantly hiked salaries and pensions of Central government employees. Significantly, Rao and Vajpayee despite better economic performances could not win re-elections after their full terms in the offices.

Before MGNREGA was unveiled for whole of India in 2005, its various predecessors bearing several names had accounted for $18 billion in three decades. In the next eight years, the government would spend roughly about $40 billion in implementing rural employment guarantee scheme. It is implemented at the level of Gram Panchayats with no involvement of contractors and is meant for unskilled labour. The scheme provided for a statutory guarantee of 100 days of works a year. India's top auditor, the Comptroller and Auditor General (CAG), in its performance audit in 2012 raised serious questions in the manner in which it was implemented. But the Congress, which swore by the name of MGNREGA in the times of UPA-I, would push the scheme more aggressively, with the belief that it had given the party an electoral victory, after the party returned to form the UPA-II (2009-14).

But the scheme on the grounds was a story of gross loot. And beneficiaries were not the poor, but a new class, which arrived on the scene as rural political leaders, who would pocket most of the money and show off their riches in villages and elsewhere.

Bihar was heading for the Assembly elections in 2010, and the RJD chief Lalu Prasad had called a meeting of party leaders holding positions in Panchayats as 'Mukhiya' and 'Sarpanch'. He could not believe the sight of SUVs lined up on both sides of his Tughlaq Road bungalow in New Delhi. Panchayat leaders had zipped in to New Delhi in their swanky SUVs. The RJD chief realized that a new crop of political leaders had arrived on the scene with strong financial muscles. They sought to climb the ladder to higher levels in politics. They were beneficiaries of ill-gotten money made through fictitious works carried out under the MGNREGA.

The scheme helped petty politicians amass envious wealth. At an annual conference of Panchayati Raj held at Vigyan Bhavan in New Delhi in 2013, Union ministers kept staring at rural women leaders attending the meet. It was not that they were too beautiful to attract the gaze of ministers, but for the fact that they were loaded with heavy gold jewelry. That's what the MGNREGA has done, a Union minister would say.

The state governments loved the scheme. It came handy when the ruling parties in states needed to mobilize people for their political meets or rallies, as they could pay them off from the MGNREGA wage account. And the loot would be such that the fund under the scheme would be excessively exploited during the election times. During the 2012 Uttar Pradesh Assembly elections, there were hundreds of poor gathered at a small rural party office of the BSP near Fizabad. The party flags with elephant symbol embossed on them were mounted on their bicycles. When inquired from where they had come, those 'party workers' confided being actually the MGNREGA labourers, promised to be paid a day salary under the scheme for taking part in the political rally.

The Ministry of Rural Development, which administered the scheme, would mine success stories from the states to show off that it was doing a world of good for the poor and marginal farmers. A study done in Maharashtra claimed that the MGNREGA helped history-sheeters and criminals to lead normal lives. Afforestation and reclaiming barren land for farming would be the common theme of such success stories.

Besides the MGNREGA, the Congress wanted similar programme, which could stand as an electoral insurance for the party when the UPA-II stood mired in scams. It looked at giving a makeover to National Rural Livelihoods Mission and Sonia launched 'Aajivika' in Banswara near Udaipur in Rajsthan with much fanfare in 2011. The programme sought to make rural poor stand on their feet and was modelled on Self-Help Groups (SHGs) movement, which had been quite successful in South India, particularly in Andhra Pradesh, Kerala, and Tamil Nadu. Reports suggested that the SHG campaign had formed good bases in Bihar, Odisha, Chhatisgarh, and Jammu and Kashmir.

'Aajivika' was hailed as a political avatar of the MGNREGA for the UPA-II. But not much time was lost when the realization dawned that the 'Aajivika' would be quite an arduous exercise and painfully long to become a mass movement to allow the ruling party to reap political dividends in the immediate future. Once the realization set in, the government left it to the ways of the bureaucracy with a few letters exchanged with the state governments soliciting their help in establishing necessary infrastructure. The government's contributions in the 'Aajivika' campaign were in the forms of a few conferences and workshops. It still stays on an auto-pilot mode.

The Congress began looking for big pro-poor ideas, which could fetch votes. The caucus of the NGOs in the National Advisory Council (NAC), headed by Sonia, pieced together National Food Security Bill to provide near free foodgrains to 75 per cent population in rural and 50 per cent in urban areas. Under the scheme, 25 kg of grains would be given to each family, with rice costing Rs 3 a kg, wheat Rs 2 a kg, and millet Rs 1 a kg.

KV Thomas, who was the Minister for food and consumer affairs in UPA-II, became the man to pilot the proposal. When asked how the government could seek to further balloon the food subsidy burden to almost twice the size from the current level, he would have a quick answer. 'The government gives a lot of subsidy to the corporate to the tune of billions of dollars each year through relaxation in taxes and cheaper assets (spectrum, coal, etc.). So, why can't we give a similar relief to the poor?' The argument was circular, but true. The corporate was beneficiary of underpricing of precious assets given to them. Under the Narendra Modi government, auction of a mere 22 coal-blocks would fetch a whopping $35 billion to be realized over the years. The same would happen in the case of spectrum auction.

The Congress had taken inspiration for such a food programme from the electoral successes of the Navin Patnaik led BJD in Odisha and the Raman Singh headed BJP government in Chhatisgarh. People in the two states have rewarded ruling parties for running an efficient public food distribution system (PDS) under which large sections of their population get 35 kg of rice each month at Rs 1 a kg. With enough vegetables growing in their neighbourhood, the poor relished the scheme. They do not have to worry about hunger. Both the chief ministers are comfortably placed in their respective states. The Congress sought to replicate their successes at the national level. The top brass of the Congress believed it could be electorally a game-changer.

The Manmohan Singh Cabinet cleared the proposal despite half the ministers opposing the idea. It was later enacted by the Parliament, with Opposition parties going with the government for fear of popular backlash against them. The cost would be so huge that the next government under Modi even after a year and a half in the office would keep extending the date from which it would be implemented. At the time of discussion in the Parliament, the government claimed the initial cost to implement the scheme would be $20 billion a year. But such an estimate was quite conservative and did not include other costs. Officials in the government would peg the cost to about $32 billion a year. 'The actual cost of implementing will be $25 billion a year. If you add the cost to ramp up facilities like storage, irrigation, etc., overall expenses will be $32 billion a year.' The official missed an important feature of the food procurement in India under which the government raises minimum support prices (MSP) of paddy and wheat roughly by 10 per cent each year to keep the farmer lobby happy, which would add another $4 billion to the overall cost. It would also suck in a whopping 62 million tons of food grains out of the market, leaving a potential trail of food inflation and thus hurting the middle class hard.

The government argued that the beneficiaries would have savings of $700 a year. What was not mentioned that the middle class and others would have to forego roughly $1500 a year to bear the cost spike of food grains' prices. The game of taking something from one set of people to others was quite old in the scheme of things of the Congress!

In the last 66 years, the war against poverty has been fought with blunted weapons. Poor stayed firmly into vicious cycle of poverty, while those with political connections shared the loot of public money meant for anti-poverty schemes. The poor had much daunting task at their hands to manage two meals a day to understand the 'politics of poverty' practiced by the Congress ostensibly for their welfare.

As spokes they spun for their lives, with much larger wheel of the 'politics of poverty' rolling on years after years to keep the Congress firmly in the power.

Subsequent revelations of scams after scams paralyzed the government beyond redemption. Indian quest to redeem its polity and economy was in shambles. Cynicism spread far and wide. People, bureaucracy, and business men turned cynical. Bureaucrats stopped taking decisions and files kept moving back and forth. Businessmen sought opportunities outside India. Capital and enterprises became foreign bound. Indian economy looked doomed. The political class was everyone's whipping boy. The stage was set for someone to retrieve India from the abyss.

Modi had been watching the power play in New Delhi for quite long. He had the best of credentials among the second generation of leaders within the BJP. He began preparation much before his rivals got into the comfort zones. He had his script ready much before he had to share it with his audience. He had to emerge as one who could instill hope. He had to shield bureaucrats to make them take decisions. Redemption lied in top leadership not being afraid of the consequences of decisions. The duality of power center had given a body blow to the governance. The time was ripe for a leader to dawn who could demolish such duality and redeem the sanctity of the PMO.

The spectacles of the anti-corruption activist Anna Hazare movement at Jantar Mantar and iconic Ramlila Ground in New Delhi had filled the air with toxic negativism. The Congress was doomed even before the nation went to the polls.

The socialists were discredited for squandering people's trust on earlier occasions for their petty self-interests. Modi harvested the crop of negativism. His deeds to attract businesses in Gujrat were by then tales of folklores. His disdain for politics of poverty enthused the masses. India was enchanted by the communication wizardry of Modi.

He drew crowds in hundreds of thousands. In south of the Vindhyanchal (South India), Modi got audiences who heard him in attention and with admiration. Television beamed his speeches round the clock. The office-goers left instructions at home to record his speeches so as to watch them in leisure. India's thirst for a speaking leader seemed quenched. After Nehru and Vajpayee, India had found a leader who had his own mind. And he emerged the principal challenger to the politics of poverty. He would seek to unveil blueprints in gradual manner to guide India from a welfare state to an enabling state where the politics of poverty would be relegated to the oblivion and in place would seek to enable the poor to stand on their feet.

The enabler Narendra Modi had arrived on the scene.

The Burning House

RAHUL Gandhi has been more of a submarine politician, spending most of the times away from the public glare, and occasionally surfacing to splash the political waters.

More than a decade has gone by since Rahul entered the political arena. Heir to the largest political party in India, Rahul is yet to reverse the Congress' fortune of sliding down the hill. With the Congress' fate tied to Rahul's political stock, Indian politics is witnessing a political vacuum in the Opposition space. When Modi launched frontal attack on the Congress in the run up to the 2014 Lok Sabha elections, Rahul's leadership skills were exposed to the extent of embarrassment for his party leaders. He was found woefully short of ideas to lift the morale of the Congress workers.

After more than one and a half decades the Congress is on the cusp of a generational change in the leadership. Rahul is set to take the mantle of the Congress leadership from his mother. The BJP already went with the generational change after much of the upheaval to settle down to a powerful leadership under Modi. The Congress true to its character of being status-quoist is delaying the eventual transition at a heavy cost.

In his more than a decade in politics, Rahul has attempted to slip into various roles, including that of an angry man. He's still searching for an identity. He has tried hard. His fast graying beard bears proof of his efforts. He shot to the fame, if at all there is any, by his maiden speech in Lok Sabha (2008) during the no-trust vote against the Manmohan Singh led UPA-I government on the issue of Indo-US nuclear deal when he talked of Sasikala and Kalawati. They were two women he had met in the Vidarbha region of Maharashtra. He told their stories of poverty. He told the packed House, that nuclear energy would bring such women out of poverty, and dream of their sons to become an IAS, engineer and corporate executive could possibly come true. After the speech, the women would have their own share of fame and local congress leaders would pour money in their coffers in their bid for Rahul to take note of them. Poverty of marginal farmers in the Vidarbha region, known world over for farmers' suicide, would only deepen in times to come.

Rahul would fancy having meals and staying at places of Dalit (scheduled castes) in Uttar Pradesh. He along with his foreign bred advisers would make it a point to regularly stay at Dalit hamlets in Uttar Pradesh. A year later (2009), Rahul brought the then British foreign secretary David Miliband for an overnight stay at a Dalit woman Shivkumari's village Simara in his Parliamentary constituency Amethi on a day when the state celebrated birth day of the Dalit queen and the then chief minister Mayawati. Miliband was like those foreigners who are in love with India and seek to discover the country by staying at night at villages, particularly of poorest of the poor. Many before him have done so and wrote books to portray India with their respective biases.

Scion of the Gandhi dynasty showed off his friend list to the poor people in the Simara village, which despite being his family constituency for ages, was deep into poverty. Rahul was trying a marriage of poverty tourism with the 'Dalit' politics. But Miliband did become a name known to most of the politicians in Uttar Pradesh. The state chief minister Akhilesh Yadav would make a point to inquire whether Miliband won or lost elections in his country, and when told that "he lost one", he would be mighty pleased.

The year 2009 was quite a good one for Rahul and his only taste of success. The Congress led UPA won re-elections. Manmohan Singh was sworn in as Prime Minister one more time. The UPA-II was unveiled. The Congress won as many as 22 Lok Sabha seats in Uttar Pradesh where the party was written off by all the political pundits.

As far as Uttar Pradesh is concerned, the electoral battle was between Rahul and Akhilesh. Samajwadi Party and Congress had an identical score in the verdict of the 2009 Lok Sabha elections. Yet, Rahul was a winner and Akhilesh emerged a loser, because latter's party strength had slumped from 36 to 22. Rahul was hailed as a 'young' Congress leader having delivered strong political punches in a tough battle. Akhilesh would soon go over 35 years of age and he would request: 'Please do not call me a young leader once I cross 35'. Rahul is at least seven years older to him.

The two would soon be locked in another electoral battle, which would catch attention of the whole country. In the 2009 elections, Akhilesh had won from both Kannauj and Firozabad Lok Sabha constituencies and as per the rule he had to vacate one. He vacated Firozabad, which is a manufacturing base of bangles. Rahul and Akhilesh are a lot similar. Both are heirs to their respective political dynasties. Akhilesh's father Mulayam Singh Yadav like Sonia was ageing.

But there was a difference. Unlike the Gandhi dynasty in which the only mother-son duo are in politics, the whole Mulayam clan is there from the state Assembly to Indian Parliament as MLAs and MPs. At least eight members of the Mulayam Clan are either in the Indian Parliament or in the Uttar Pradesh Assembly. So, when Akhilesh vacated Firozabad Lok Sabha seat, his wife -- Dimple Yadav -- stepped out of the Yadav family home.

The Gandhis and Yadavs had one unwritten pact that they never campaigned against each other when their family members were contesting elections. But Rahul broke the rule and invited open challenge from Akhilesh. Quite a few actors from the Indian film industry with some political connections had dabbled into politics in the past. Indian politics is quite warm to absorb film actors. Raj Babbar was one of them. His political career till then had been in Mulayam's shadow. But he quit Samajwadi Party to join the Congress during the political upheaval caused by the Indo-US nuclear deal in 2008. He deserted Mulayam because of his differences with Amar Singh, who called shots in the Samajwadi Party and could snub any, including those from the Yadav family. The Congress fielded him against Dimple. He was up against the family honour of the Yadav family.

Akhilesh had not yet cemented his position fully in his party and had many detractors among politically strong uncles. At that time Azam Khan was seen as tallest leader of Muslims in the state and was at war with Amar Singh. Azam was sulking after being sidelined from the affairs of the party. Babbar and Azam made a common cause. Azam stayed behind the doors and swung Muslim votes in Firozabad for Babbar. Amar Singh would be away from the thick of affairs following his kidney transplant operation in Singapore. His absence would mean that Dimple would be deprived of monetary muscle to crush Azam's subtle designs.

A day before the verdict of the bypoll, Akhilesh would say, Dimple would win, but with thin margin. When told that the Congress leader Digvijay Singh was betting on Babbar's win, Akhilesh would sound emotionally distraught. 'The amount of money that Raj Babbar has distributed in Firozabad is beyond imagination.' he would say.

Dimple lost the byelections. Akhilesh was furious and wounded. Rahul basked in the glory of having hunted a lion in his den. The Congress leaders further ballooned Rahul's success. Akhilesh would not lose time to declare a war on Rahul. 'Now onward, elections in Uttar Pradesh will be fought between Rahul Gandhi and me,' he would say.

In another three years, Uttar Pradesh hosted a big electoral battle to decide who would rule the state. Akhilesh would use the opportunity to emerge out of his father's shadow. His bicycle yatras (marches) to nook and corner of the state would connect him with the youth. He coined the term 'berozgar baap (unemployed father)'. Large sections of the youth were unemployed and burdened with the task to feed family without assured means of income. Akhilesh learnt that the people in the state were angry with the Mayawati government and ready for a change. He came up with the ideas of unemployment allowances for 'berozgar baap' and laptop for school going students. His father added his pet subject, 'waiver of the farm loan'.

Rahul in contrast ranted that money sent by Central government to the state was devoured by 'elephant' in Lucknow. Elephant is the election symbol of the BSP and a number of ministers of the Mayawati Cabinet were mired in scams unearthed by the state Lokayukta. Rahul listed problems sans solutions. He would slip into the role of an angry 'young' man. He would roll up his sleeves and tear apart manifesto of Akhilesh's party at election rallies.

But with three ideas, Samajwadi Party uprooted Mayawati's BSP from power in Lucknow. The Congress was decimated. Akhilesh had taken a sweet revenge over Rahul. He emerged as youth icon in the state. Rahul would not learn any lesson. He would meet people, but would not find solutions. He would stay in the 'angry young man' mode for a while.

On November 4, 2012, a good nine months after embarrassing electoral loss in Uttar Pradesh, Rahul addressed a public rally at Ramlila Ground in Delhi. He enacted his role of an angry man. 'Maen jaantaa hun ki aap log system se tang aa chuke haen...aap log system maen change chaahate haen...maen aapke saath iske liye khada hun (I know, you all are fed up with the system, and want a change, and I am standing with you'.

Rahul would position himself as a change agent in the presence of the then Prime Minister Manmohan Singh, Sonia and all top guns of the party. By then he had opened the doors within the Youth Congress for new people who were out of the political system. At the same venue, he would say 'Congress was a party of a dozen people until Mahatma Gandhi opened its door for the mass, and afterwards the British ran away in a matter of few years'.

Rahul gave a sense that he was inspired by the Mahatma. He, however, unknowingly exposed his poor knowledge of history of Indian freedom struggle. The Congress was quite a force to reckon with by the time the Mahatma had arrived on the scene. The Congress was surely not a party of a dozen leaders by the time Mahatma 'opened the door for the masses'. The Congress was already an engine of millions of people pursuing the path of freedom. A basic government sanctioned history book for secondary schools would have clarified the misconception of Rahul. Yet, he blared his ignorance with a lot of bravado.

In those days, he was also trying to buy the title of the 'Young India', which the Mahatma's weekly newspaper in South Africa. As the Mahatma sought to familiarize with conditions of the poor in India after he returned from South Africa, Rahul also attempted doing so and even after more than a decade in politics he continues to do so.

Senior Congress leaders would say Rahul was too much into idealism. His blueprint for revival of the Congress was too futuristic and there were no answers to immediate challenges. The Congress was faced with the prospect of a strong challenger in Modi in the immediate future and Rahul talked of structure and processes of the party.

Within the party he was seen stricken by the American model of politics. He began experimenting with the idea of 'preliminaries' to pick candidates for party tickets in elections. He employed the same idea in elections for positions in the Youth Congress. He sought to extend the idea in the Congress as well. Party leaders would say the idea would only breed enmity at the grassroots level among the Congress workers. But the 'power-point' presentation ways of politics stayed with Rahul.

In his limited public discourses, Rahul gave fair impression that he's in love with theories. His articulation of various subjects through illustrations like -- 'escape velocity' for Dalits; 'India is not an elephant, but a beehive'; 'power is poison'; 'poverty is a state of mind' -- suggests one thing, that Rahul is excessively spoon-fed. And those who spoon feed him have surely not seen rural India at all. His articulation of subjects in such manners has left his audiences baffled on occasions and even to the extent of splitting the hairs.

Rahul held some 'off the record' interactions with the print media at his Tughlaq Lane residence in New Delhi. After each such interactions, he would strictly make a point to state that nothing of what he spoke of should come in the print in any form. Later, journalists would be left with no reason or incentive to attend such interactions. A lot of them were already fatigued to have been 'dragged' to Amethi in SUVs zipping through highways at excessive speed, with scribes having their hearts in their mouths on such journeys.

Politics is an art. But for Rahul, politics is science. He spent years shepherding the Youth Congress, but when the time came to show political impact at the times of elections, it proved to be a pigmy.

Dalits in Uttar Pradesh stayed away from the Congress and sections of the youth among them saw virtues in Modi's promises of development. More than rhetoric, Dalit youths wanted jobs and better living conditions. Mayawati had ensured a sense of security for them. They wanted to climb little more on the ladder of economic security. Other than Mahatma Gandhi National Rural Employment Guarantee Scheme (MGREGS), Rahul did not have much to offer. They knew that the MGNREGS was meant for distress employment. It would just allow them to survive. They wanted a deal beyond mere survival.

Rahul's ultra-Leftism with his proactive engagement at Dalit hamlets and Tribal places where he opposed land acquisition for big industries gave a telling blow to the Congress, with the party losing appeal among middle class and aspirational sections of the society. Rahul's activism against industries would project his image of an 'anti-development' politician, who was yet to offer an alternative model of economic progress of the country. Rahul could not win over Dalits and tribal for his party. They loved his coming to their places, but when times came to cast their votes the Congress was hardly in the minds.

Rahul robbed legitimacy of the Manmohan Singh government by sticking to his 'change the system mode'. His ideas of change within the Congress created more confusion than cohesion. Elders in the party looked dejected, while the young lot rallied behind him in anticipation of quick gains in the form of climbing up the political ladder.

When the time came for the big stage to lock horns with Modi, Rahul looked dwarfed. It was a contest of unequal. One spoke for hours holding his audience engaged and interested. The other fumed and fumbled. The audience wondered what the anger was for when his party had ruled the country for most parts of the Independent history. Subsequently, the size of Rahul's election rallies got smaller and smaller. And when elections came closer, people were tough to find to attend rallies addressed by Rahul.

It became Herculean task for Congress leaders to mobilize people in his rallies. The Congress managers got a few 'stage-managed' television interviews for him. Rahul would be repetitive in his answers despite helpful and patient interviewers searching for meaning in his utterances. No matter what the question asked, his answers would be more or less the same, with a few words juggled here and there.

With Sonia not keeping well in the run up to the elections and Manmohan Singh having bid farewell to politics much before he self-excluded from the race of the next Prime Minister, Rahul led Congress in the 2014 Lok Sabha elections. And Modi found the Congress a sitting duck. The party was decimated with ease. The Congress looked rudderless.

The sudden bankruptcy in the Congress was on account of a move which happened a couple of years before the landmark 2014 elections. Pranab Mukherjee had exited from the active politics. He went away by taking the only available reward for his contributions to the Congress in a long and illustrious career. And that reward was a five year stay at the top of the Raisina Hills, which oversaw the Indian Parliament and South and North Blocks in the vicinity.

India's 13th President by all accounts is the most astute politician alive in the country. His understanding of politics is impeccable. Those who heard his speeches in Parliament during his times as an MP and Minister know that the current 16th Lok Sabha is a lot poorer, because there is none who can speak like him. None can recall the Constitutional nuances with such ease to make Parliamentary debates worthy of researches for the posterity.

With Advani on the 'mute' mode despite being in the Lok Sabha and Mukherjee in the Rashtrapati Bhavan, generational shift in the contemporary politics too has taken both the Houses of Parliament in its ambit. Mukherjee was short-tempered, yet destroyer of the Opposition. His critics slammed him being India's worst Finance Minister ever, but they never disputed his standing in the Parliamentary history of India. He argued for building and protecting institutions. 'Indian democracy is vibrant because of its institutions,' he would say. When the NGOs (Non-Governmental Organizations) launched frontal attack on the established political system, it would be Mukherjee who would make the spirited defence of the institutions and warn people of adverse consequences of belittling them.

But fate is seemingly more relevant in politics than in any other fields, and it's no surprise that most of the successful politicians in the country often keep one such fortune-teller in their companies. Mukherjee's political career was nothing short of a spectacular and breathtaking tale. He became Finance Minister of India at an age of 46, which remains a feat not yet scaled by any. But the crown of Indian politics eluded him and that was becoming Prime Minister of the country.

He was best suited to be India's Prime Minister in 2004. Yet, Sonia chose Manmohan Singh. Her choice was politically correct to keep the interests of the Gandhi dynasty intact. She must have known that Mukherjee would not have just been a Prime Minister with no control over the party. Prime Ministers in India have always commanded strong political leadership. Manmohan Singh proved an exception.

But history of the Congress under Rao and Sitaram Keshri was not yet forgotten; at least by the coterie surrounding Sonia. The fear was quite alive that a non-Gandhi Prime Minister could undermine legacy of the dynasty. The choice fell on Manmohan Singh. He was an economist in a bureaucrat's skin. He did not understand politics or feigned not to have any interest. His loyalty was to his benefactor. The office of Prime Minister never became stronger than that of the Congress president. Manmohan Singh was robbed off all legitimacy of his office by Rahul at the end of the tenure of the UPA-II. Heir to the Gandhi dynasty indulged in political stunts often, which would only ridicule the office of the Prime Minister. Still, Manmohan Singh's loyalty to Sonia was not an ounce less.

Had it been Mukherjee leading the UPA governments for a decade, India's sorry tale of a ship adrift on the high sea may have had a different script. The UPA governments lacked an anchor to steady the ship in turbulent waters. India came to terms with harsh political reality at an exorbitant cost, that the Prime Minister must be a strong politician.

In flashback, Advani sought to tell people in the 2009 elections, that there was heavy cost in having a 'weak' Prime Minister. His election campaign theme was anchored on the 'weak' Prime Minister premise. Advani explained that the stronger centre of power existed in 10, Janpath. An extra-Constitutional authority calling shots in a government elected by the people through democratic ways would only undermine interests of the nation. India was, however, not ready to listen to Advani's tales. People rejected him. But they believed the same tale when told by Modi five years later.

Politics is full of ironies. Advani campaigned in 2009 on issues of 'weak Prime Minister', a parallel economy of black money belittling progress of the country, and massive outflow of ill-gotten money into tax havens abroad, besides price rise breaking back of the middle class and poor alike. Five years later, Modi destroyed the Congress on same issues in such lethal ways that people would not only reject the Gandhi dynasty but change the script of Indian politics in ways not anticipated by any acclaimed political pundits.

Advani surely spoke of issues before their times had arrived. A full ramification of the flight of the capital in the form of black money abroad was not an idea, which struck chord with the people. A month after the 2009 verdict, Kalyan Singh, who was chief minister of Uttar Pradesh (1991-92, 1997-99) and elected to Lok Sabha in 2009 elections from Etah as an Independent, would say that the whole Advani campaign was flawed. 'The nation knew Manmohan Singh as an honest and knowledgeable person. Advani's personal attack on him would not have struck chord with the people. Price rise is an issue which can never become an election plank, because poor in rural areas are not affected by it in manners the middle class suffer in metropolitan cities. And the issue of black money was too vague for the people to relate to,' Kalyan Singh called 'Babu ji'' by his followers would say.

Politics and the game of chess are a lot similar. Some of the moves have lethal consequences. They set off trappings, which are understood by the time the game is over. Four months before the Congress had to seek fresh mandate in May 2009, Mukherjee took a significant decision. He abandoned his Ministry of External Affairs. In January 2009, he sought and got portfolio of the Finance Ministry. He complained of pains of frequent foreign tours and took the alibi of his health conditions to claim the Ministry of Finance. P Chidambaram was edged out of his abode.

Lawyer turned politicians often take fancy that they are best suited to become Finance Ministers. Their forte of deductive logical reasoning comes handy when it comes to explain economic issues. Arun Jaitely is also smitten with similar bug. Chidambaram in the Ministry of Home Affairs was a sulking soul. He coveted Finance Ministry. He would sulk until Mukherjee made his next move. But that would be three years later. Until his next move, Mukherjee carved out autonomous functioning of the Ministry of Finance and presented Union Budgets, which hardly had the stamp of Manmohan Singh. Members of the Manmohan Singh Cabinet took clues from Mukherjee and sought to ape him. Soon, Singh's writ did not run even within his Cabinet.

Power of corridors in New Delhi would buzz with gossips of a tug of war between Mukherjee and Chidambaram, and that they were not on talking terms. In two years' time (2011), the chewing bug controversy would play out wherein the intelligence agencies allegedly planted hearing devices in Mukherjee's office. Fracas between the two leaders would come to such an extent that Singh would need to mediate and broker peace. Peace would be brokered, but the world would know that Singh headed the most discordant and incoherent Cabinet.

Mukherjee's next move came in 2012. It came at a time when the street agitation against the government had become norms of the day. Scams were tumbling out of the closet. Ministers scored self-goals often. Air smelt of negativism. Mukherjee exited politics. He took a flight uphill from the North Block to the Rashtrapati Bhavan. None would lay the path for him to walk into the majestic Raisina Hill palace. He would make his own journey.

Much before Presidential elections would become a topic of discussions and speculation in the press, Mukherjee would share his 'thought' to walk in the lawns of the Rashtrapati Bhavan with his 'coterie' of editors and media heads. The UPA-II was a Group of Ministers' (GoM) government. Mukherjee carried burdens disproportionate to human abilities. Sonia had an alibi not to spare him for his Raisina Hill aims. But more than the issue of government responsibilities, Sonia weighed the idea of a Muslim President, with her eyes set on minority vote base. She preferred Vice-President Hamid Ansari.

Trinamool Congress supremo Mamata Banerjee made Sonia's thoughts public, that Ansari was her number one choice and Pranab 'Da' the second. She was still an alliance partner of the UPA and was part of the government. Sonia had a brief consultation with her over the upcoming Presidential elections. The consultation was limited to Banerjee asking Sonia's choices. She held grudges against Mukherjee. True to his short-tempered nature, Mukherjee is said to have snubbed Banerjee in one Cabinet meeting when she was still the Minister for Railways in such a manner that she had been full of tears afterwards. Hearing the name of Mukherjee as one of the two choices, Banerjee would literally explode and offer herself as a potential candidate for the post to the waiting media outside the 10, Janpath. When left with no option and forced to yield to the issue of a Bengali pride, Trinamool Congress 'halfheartedly' extended support to Mukherjee. But that would be not before the temperamental leader would showcase her dramatic skills in New Delhi.

Mukherjee was a political veteran of many seasons. Knowing well that no such offer would come his ways, he staked claim on the high Constitutional post within the party. Banerjee upped the ante. She went to Samajwadi Party chief Mulayam Singh Yadav. They jointly 'proposed' Manmohan Singh's name as potential candidate for elections to the post of India's next President. They together put Sonia in the spot. Banerjee is politically a street fighter. She is not bothered much about the art of politicking. She thinks straight and talks straight.

Mulayam and Banerjee are contrasting political characters and would always make for unnatural friends. He's broken all records of U-turns in Indian politics. He will say something and do something else. He played his parts for his 'friend' Mukherjee. Sonia vacillated or showed off being in conditions of Hamlet's dilemma. She agreed on Mukherjee's name afterward.

Mulayam would go on records, saying he pressured the Congress to declare Mukherjee's name. He would not say that he might just have acted out his role from the script drafted by Mukherjee. Banerjee was stumped. She would subsequently keep distance with Mulayam and his party and later begin thinking beyond the Third Front. Privately, her party MPs would say that they would not have any truck with Mulayam until he snapped all relations with the Left parties.

Sonia's decision for Mukherjee was halfhearted. Neither she nor Manmohan Singh took the pain to seek support of the BJP in the Presidential elections. Mukherjee was denied the honour of being a unanimously elected President of India.

Purno Sangma popped out as a challenger of Mukherjee with the support of Navin Patnaik led Biju Janta Dal, which eyed the tribal vote base in doing so, and the BJP, which opposed the nominee of the ruling party on a matter of principle, that no support was sought from the largest Opposition party before the name was made public, backed him. 'If Prime Minister or Sonia had called Advani even a minute before making Mukherjee's name public, the BJP would have been more than happy to support him in the elections,' JD (U) chief Sharad Yadav later said.

In November 2012, when Mukherjee took the Raisina Hill flight, the Congress was pushed to the wall. The BJP had not yet found its leader. The saffron party was in the midst of a fratricidal war among the second generation leaders. They all were plotting their next moves. The RSS had not yet found ways to break the New Delhi caucus within the BJP. The Nitish Kumar led JD (U) was still an ally of the BJP. This party from the socialist camp took the first step to think independently of the BJP and decided to support Mukherjee in the Presidential elections. None dared say in those times that the BJP could on its own register a majority in the Lok Sabha in the elections due in less than two years. The consensus opinion in New Delhi was that there would be a fractured mandate. No party or the alliances in current forms – the UPA and the NDA -- would get a majority on its own.

Anticipating Constitutional challenges in 2014 as 'people will not give a clear verdict', the socialist block was the cheer-leader of Mukherjee. 'He knows the Constitution and only he can deal with situations arising out of instability in 2014,' Sharad Yadav would say, while explaining why despite his party being in the NDA was backing a Congress nominee.

Nitish became the buzzword for potential PM candidate. A few of leaders within the BJP would further bloat his ego and make him seriously think about his chances of becoming the Prime Minister. The idea of the Third Front was not yet dead. Regional parties were ruling large number of the states. Samajwadi Party (Uttar Pradesh), JD (U) (Bihar), Trinamool (West Bengal), Biju Janata Dal (Odisha), DMK (Tamil Nadu), and Shiromani Akali Dal (Punjab) gave ample strength of regional parties in Indian politics, besides the newly carved out Telangana and residual state of Andhra Pradesh surrendered to the regional parties by acts of sheer opportunism by the Congress. Their strength was only on the rise. This trend further crushed the idea that the BJP led NDA, which was consisting of just four smaller parties, would cobble up a majority of its own in the Lok Sabha.

Banerjee's political ambitions were soaring. She had just a year before created history and achieved a feat by uprooting 34 long years of the Left rule in West Bengal. She was struck by the political bug, which had bitten Mayawati before in the 2009 elections. Banerjee seriously thought of winning 100 Lok Sabha seats and thus become a rallying point for all regional forces in the country. She suitably floated the idea of Federal Front. 'India will be ruled not from New Delhi, but from the state capitals,' she would often say. Her party leaders by then had known for better, that only one voice spoke in Trinamool and that was of 'Didi'. She had quit the Congress to float her own party. Though she had quit the party where sycophancy was institutionalized, she carried the virus to her new political outfit and unveiled its much magnified version. None in Trinamool blessed with political senses dared bring sanity in the thoughts of 'Didi'. Her MPs in New Delhi would take names of states with any Bengali population to claim electoral potential of Trinamool. Delhi, Jharkhand, Odisha, North-east were states commonly referred to by Trinamool leaders, who in later days also added Uttar Pradesh and Bihar in their list.

Mulayam's dream of becoming Prime Minister was intact. He would ask his audience in his public rallies in Uttar Pradesh -- 'when will you make me Prime Minister of India'. All that he needed to turn his dream into reality was 50 odd Lok Sabha seats in the kitty of his party and a fractured mandate. If these three aspirants for the post of Prime Minister were not enough, J Jayalalitha of the AIADMK in Tamil Nadu too believed the time had come for her to play a big role in the national politics. She also wanted a shot at the top executive post in the event of a fractured event.

There were at least four candidates for the post of Prime Minister who began making moves after Mukherjee occupied the top Constitutional post. Hopes had taken such firm wings that they were too eager to fly, and Nitish made the first move. With an ashen-looking Sharad on his side, Nitish snapped 17 years old alliance with the BJP (June, 2013). Sharad was well aware that the ground reports from Bihar were not in sync with grandiose positioning of his ambitious chief minister.

Nitish had his one in Third Front and another in the Federal Front. Sharad knew by then that he would not even win his Lok Sabha constituency from Madhepura, known as 'Rome of Gope (Yadavs)', without the support of the BJP. Even while the state unit of the BJP never challenged the leadership of Nitish, he snapped the ties, without spelling reasons. Personal interests outweighed political realities. That happened within seven months of Mukherjee becoming President of India and set off a yearlong election campaign at the end of which people were not tired but fired with dreams of prosperity.

Mukherjee becoming President was seen as signal for political instability ahead. Third Front and Federal Front were toasts of political commentaries. The Congress was staring into an uncertain future. The party leaders began 'thinking aloud' of virtue in staying out of power for some time. Nine out of 10 Congressmen would say, 'the party needs to be out of power for some time'. When Sonia was still in her 'to be or not to be' dilemma over giving nod to Mukherjee's name, the Congress leaders would not mind indulging in thought, that 'Manmohan Singh should retire and for the services that he has done for the party he has his legitimate claims on Raisina Hill abode'. Singh was thought best suited to serve interests of the Gandhi family in the event of political instability after the elections.

The idea of a 'stop-gap arrangement' was also in the air. Mukherjee could become Prime Minister till elections and 'wash off' accumulated 'taint' of scams attached to the ruling UPA alliance. This way the Congress could attempt to climb out of the 'self-dug' grave in which the party had fallen. 'Mukherjee could be Prime Minister for two years. Even if the Congress is routed in 2014, Rahul can concentrate on Mission 2019 with free hand. He will be about 49 years of age by then and would have gained enough political experience.' Congress' best bait was a few years of political instability following which the party could stage a comeback. They still thought on times when Rajiv was ousted in 1989 and the Congress staged a comeback to power in 1991. But these were 'wishful' thinking.

Mukherjee's exit from the government and the party brought down the facade of defence they had enjoyed under India's next President. The Opposition would tear apart the government in Parliament and outside. The government sub-grouped among factions which sparred regularly. Chidambaram returned to his coveted post of Finance Minister. He would attempt changing the gear of the UPA government to unveil strong doze of reforms.

Americans were particularly impatient with the government not pushing 100 per cent Foreign Direct Investment in the multi-brand retail. Incidentally, Mukherjee had gone to the US when he was still Finance Minister of India. The moment he checked in his hotel there, the phone rang in his room. To his hello, a lady on the other side said: 'I am Hillary Clinton, Secretary of the State...just wanted to know when the FDI in multi-brand retail would be cleared by your government.' Quite taken aback by the extra-ordinary interest shown by the US government, Mukherjee excused himself, saying that he was on a private visit to her country and such matters could be discussed on a later date.

Manmohan Singh may have bothered least about his image in India, but he was quite touchy about his perception in the US. He had walked extra miles to show he was enamoured with the US. Even if 75 per cent of the people in India did not know who was Geroge Bush, Manmohan Singh would tell him that Indians loved him. Barack Obama's penchant to call Singh a 'wise' man was always music to ears for the man in blue turban.

With Chidambaram back in the Ministry of Finance, Singh would take fast measures to please his American audience. In a span of two days, Singh would clear ways for market linked pricing of diesel and LPG gas, besides giving nod to FDI in aviation and multi-brand retail. These decisions would force Trinamool Congress to exit the UPA-II. These decisions were taken to silence the critics who prescribed FDI in multi-brand retail as the key to unlock the prison of 'policy paralysis' in which the government was caged. The lobbyists argued that FDI in multi-brand retail would be an answer to India's woes of high inflation, unemployment, besides ensuring remunerative prices for farmers.

But that was waking up at a time when the sun was setting. The Congress looked tired and fatigued. Some of the Congress leaders quite wisely chose not to contest the 2014 Lok Sabha elections. Others jumped in the fray with a lot of reluctance. They had known what would be the 2014 verdict much in advance. Their bet was on whether the Congress would cross the 100 mark in Lok Sabha, or slip into an abyss.

The Congress was predictably pushed into an abyss.

Talking the wave

Wave in politics is seldom spontaneous.

It's built up and sustained, and eventually a decisive direction is given. It does not happen all the times. It comes on rare occasions and leave lasting imprints. Sometimes, they change the course of politics. Sometimes their imprints are as short-lived as those on sands washed off by sea waves.

The 2014 electoral battle was fought among chief ministers. None of the contenders belonged to New Delhi. They were all outsiders. Generational shift in Indian politics had robbed New Delhi of its all political splendor.

Chief Ministers in the fray competed differently. One sought mandate for development. Other pitched to preserve secular fabric of the country. Another apprehended corporate conspiracy and sought mandate for 'trickle-down theory' of development. And one even thought that there had been no Prime Minister from South India for quite a long time.

Politics of 'Hindutva' and 'Mandal' was history. People were aware of things which had become history. Political leaders, however, are victims of inertia, and are in habit of checking on people when time comes to renew their contracts for another five years during elections. But when people deliver verdict contrary to their belief, they re-position themselves.

In the battle of chief ministers, people weighed their achievements. What they had done for their respective states came under the popular scanner.

A decade of Manmohan Singh rule had given India twin jolts – jobless growth and investment drought. Politics of poverty had run full steam, and there were no more coals left for it to keep burning more. The plot was set for politics of development. It all boiled down to the developmental credentials of the competing chief ministers. People believed and listened to the one who had delivered, while others struggled for audiences.

There is a saying popular in Indian bureaucracy, which is told to all new recruits as a gospel truth. 'Your image reaches the place before you go there, and accordingly people who work with you will adjust in advance.' The 2014 battle too was all about image and perception.

The Chief Ministers -- Narendra Modi (Gujrat), Nitish Kumar (Bihar), J Jayalalitha (Tamil Nadu), and Mamata Banerjee (West Bengal) – explicitly or implicitly approached the 2014 battle with one common goal. They all carried specific and unique images which were stuck with them. Modi was a class apart from among the club of chief ministers. He was seen as a man who had led Gujrat to 'phenomenal' growth. No red-tap existed in Gujrat. Decisions were quick. Processes were in place to execute prospective projects. Industrialists did not need to wait endlessly for land to set up plants, for they were already earmarked.

Banerjee was building a campaign on the slogan of 'ma, maati, manush', which essentially was against land acquisition in West Bengal. Ratan Tata, head of the salt to software conglomerate, wanted to set up a Nano car factory in Singur in the state. Buddhadeb Bhattacharya, who was the last chief minister of the Left alliance in West Bengal, was desperately wooing industries to put his state on the path of development. Banerjee sensed an opportunity to deliver a mortal blow to the three decades old Left rule in West Bengal. The Nano car became collateral damage in political crossfire. A miffed Tata scrapped Singur project (2008).

A month later, Modi, while addressing Gujrati community in New Delhi, recalled his Singur connections. 'The moment I came to know of the decision to scrap the project, I sent an SMS to Ratan Tata, with just one word – Suswagatam (welcome).' Modi would say, he later told Tata that he could choose any place in Gujrat for the Nano car project and begin work the day he desired. Nano car factory consequently took a flight from

Singur to Sanand in Gujrat.

Tales of Modi's feats to attract businesses in Gujrat had spread far and wide. Even his rivals shared such tales. One of his political rivals recalled one such interesting anecdote. 'One Kolkata based industrialist had applied online with the state government seeking permission to set up medium sized factory in Gujrat. A day later, he got a call on his mobile phone, with the caller introducing himself -- I am Narendra Modi, the chief minister of Gujrat.' On the phone, Modi informed the industrialist of having seen his application and asked if he could fly to Gandhinagar next day to meet him. The industrialist already in utter disbelief took the first flight.

Armed with a suitcase of files and paper works, he walked into the office of the Gujrat chief minister. 'Let's not waste time in these papers. We have studied your proposal and here are five pages for MoU (Memorandum of Understanding). Please take a look and see if there is anything missing,' Modi told the awe-struck industrialist.

By the time the 2014 Lok Sabha elections neared, tales of Modi were on lips of many around the country. A boat man near Varanasi from where Modi would contest Lok Sabha elections would ask press corps, who had para-trooped in the holy city in hundred, 'is it true that none goes to bed hungry in Gujrat'. In Ghazipur near Varanasi, villagers would ask; 'is it true there is none who is unemployed in Gujrat'. Others in Uttar Pradesh would ask; 'is it true, there is no power cut in Gujrat'.

Tales of Gujrat as wonderland had not spread in Uttar Pradesh on its own. Uttar Pradesh would later account for one-fourth of BJP's strength in Lok Sabha after the elections. A meticulous preparation and extra-ordinary hard work under hawk's eyes of Modi's man Friday Amit Shah for over one year had gone into the state to make people in the state talk of wonders of Gujrat.

The BJP had appointed Shah as in-charge of the party in Uttar Pradesh a year ahead of the 2014 Lok Sabha elections. A year before Amit Shah's appointment, the BJP had suffered most humiliating drubbing in the state Assembly elections (2012). The saffron party was on its journey down the hills when the 2012 Uttar Pradesh Assembly polls took place. The party was faction-ridden, dull, and on a sick man's bed after 'Hindutva' fatigue gripped people in the state. The BJP leaders searched for opportunities elsewhere.

On the way back from the dusty town of Etawa to New Delhi where Samajwadi Party chief Mulayam Singh Yadav in the company of his Muslim mascot Azam Khan asked people to vote out the BSP supremo

Mayawati (2012), with the vehicle bouncing off too often on the road full of potholes, a bearded man dutifully refreshed occupants of the car with refreshments and provided enough stocks of snacks and cold-drinks to last for the whole journey. 'Guess, who he is," asked a Samajwadi Party leader. When told that the man was not known, the leader informed, 'he is a local BJP MLA and is joining us. Now, guess who is sending him to our party.' To another 'no idea', the replay came, 'it's one of the senior most BJP leader who lobbied with us for party ticket for him Assembly polls'.

Politicians and rats are a lot similar. They know before any of a sinking ship, and lose no time to jump off. The BJP had been in power in Uttar Pradesh two times, and Atal Bihari Vajpayee owed his stay in the 7, Race Course Road to unprecedented saffron surge in Uttar Pradesh. That tidal surge was off course due to LK Advani's 'Hindutva' turn to Indian politics in 1990s. Two decades later, Uttar Pradesh had forgotten the 'politics of Hindutva', and was left with no more appetite.

Political class in India is a gang clad in khadi and ringed khakhi. They are mostly seen with gun-toting commandos. However, it could be quite interesting to know about the most protected entity in India. On any other day, one could guess it to be one politician or the other. But those who have gone to the temple town of Ayodhya would give a different answer, that 'it's Ram Lulla'. And he does not lord over from a palace, but a small -- a little bigger than a large umbrella -- makeshift tent. He's secured by thousands of paramilitary personnel, who are armed with most sophisticated weapons found anywhere through multi-layered security rings. From the ruins of the site, which once had a medieval era mosque standing, Ram Lulla blesses visitors, pouring into the place from all parts of the country. Idols are far away from the place from where visitors have to get the 'darshan'. Devotees form serpentine queues as long as five kms to get the fleeting 'darshan' of the Lulla.

The greyish waters of the Saryu River still tells tales of Lord Rama and the epic Ramayana. The bells ring on the river-bank. Priests there besiege men and women with wings in their feet. All sins could be washed off by taking a dip in the grey waters of the River Saryu. The priests would obviously have to bless the lesser mortals with chanting of incomprehensible Shlokas to ensure their sins actually get washed off in manners that no traces would be left behind by any chance. Lord Rama shared special relationship with Kewats (Boat men). And the whole tribe of Kewats give company to the priests to take the lesser mortals mid-stream to allow them to live for moments those epochal moments of Lord Rama when he was banished by his father from the kingdom of Ayodhya. Splashing waters mid-stream on the face, one can feel one of those rare experiences when worries and pains of the moments are forgotten without any traces.

On the banks of the River one name hits the visitors hard. It's Lallu Singh. He was an MLA of the MLA from the Faizabad Assembly constituency, which includes Ayodhya. In the by-lanes of Ayodhya, visitors could come across a man riding a motorcycle with his forehead richly decorated by the religious mark 'tika'. Ayodhya is full of temples. Inhabitants live religion literally. Lanes and by-lanes ring with the chanting of the 'Dohas (couplets) of the Ramayana. Lord Rama must have not only been born here, but He would have blessed each particles to infuse life. Priests say proudly, 'Lallu Singh seeks blessings of all temples by noon as a matter of daily routine, which begins by the dawn'.

Lallu Singh had been a local MLA for over 22 years. But by the time the 2012 state Assembly elections came, he knew that large number of beautifully carved out giant pillars lying littered at various places in Ayodhya were giving ominous signs for his electoral prospects. People there had waited for ages for a majestic temple for Ram Lulla to rise in their sight and bring millions of religious tourists from across the country and abroad to change their fortunes for better. They had dreamt enough of crowds jostling to buy offerings from them. They had also dreamt of their dilapidated buildings metamorphosing into beautiful houses where people would come and stay and part with their well-earned money. The gutters flowing in the lanes and by-lanes, which bore the sight of the human and animal defecation in equal measures, would transform into well-maintained sewage system. Locals here had heard glorious tales of the economy of the places like Vaishno Devi, Tirupati, Mathura and others. Even 12-year old boys would tell with sparkle in their eyes of the prospect of Ayodhya becoming a major religious centre once the grand temple as promised by Advani and other BJP leaders in 1990s becomes a reality. Locals would accuse the BJP of having been an opportunist to have exploited the movement for the Ram temple and for having suitably forgotten once in power.

A youth leader of the Samajwadi Party – Tej Narayan Pandey alias Pawan Pandey – defeated Lallu Singh in the 2012 Assembly elections. Hindutva's last bastion had fallen. The state which propelled the BJP as a strong contender for power in New Delhi was on the verge of becoming electorally sterile. Uttar Pradesh belonged to the Samajwadi party and Bahujan Samajwadi Party of Mayawati. The BJP was in the company of the Congress, and both were not seriously taken by the people here for a shot of power in Lucknow. And, so, both the political parties lost connect with the locals. Accordingly, the BJP was handed over the worst electoral defeat in the state, with the party tally slumping to a mere 47 Assembly seats out of the 403 strength of the state Assembly (2012). But electoral fate swings and sometimes too wildly. Uttar Pradesh in another two years would re-write the political history of India.

Two years are woefully long times in politics. In February 2012, Akhilesh was a toast of the media. He had emerged a giant killer, who trounced an elephantine foe in Mayawati. Under him Samajwadi Party won a massive majority in Uttar Pradesh Assembly. Even his ageing father Mulayam Singh Yadav had not achieved such an electoral feat in his long career. Mulayam acknowledged the changed reality, and agreed to prop up his son as chief minister of the state, with little cajoling from some of his sensible advisors. When politicians grow old, they are struck by feverish zeal to ensure their sons and daughters are firmly planted in politics. Mulayam by heart is little more liberal than his contemporaries and has accordingly placed his whole clan firmly in politics. Others are happy if their sons and daughters carry their legacies. Lalu Prasad is one unhappy soul, who has not yet been successful in passing the legacy to either his son or daughter successfully.

Akhilesh had been only a member of Lok Sabha before he was sworn in as chief minister. His lack of administrative skills would soon be exposed. Within a few months, talk of the town in the state and elsewhere would be of there being not one but 'three and a half chief ministers in Uttar Pradesh'. They were Akhilesh, Mulyam, Shiv Pal Singh Yadav, and Ram Gopal Yadav (half). Bureaucrats did not pay heed to the young chief minister. They had an alibi of being pulled apart in various directions by multitude of the command centres. And, so, for two years, the only activity in the state under the young chief minister was transfer and posting of officials. Incidentally, transport and posting of officials in Uttar Pradesh is arguably the most lucrative business of the political class where they make the riches in quick time and cover their costs to contest elections just by the drop of hats.

Akhilesh would play badminton in the evening with his close friends. His aides from the days of his election campaign would become his administrative advisers. His aloofness from governance would be such that he would not even know names of his ministers. Jairam Ramesh, who was Minister of Rural Development in the UPA-II, met Akhilesh at his office in Lucknow during those days. He stroked his head when Akhilesh asked one of his aides, 'who is the rural development minister of Uttar Pradesh'. His sympathizers would say that there were so many uncles in his council of ministers that he stopped bothering about them and just let his father deal with them. His administrative honeymoon was quite extended.

The bureaucracy, which was held with an iron fist by Mayawati, suddenly loosened as if for a catharsis. The state slipped into a state of anarchy with the leadership plagued by vagueness. Goons would ride SUVs with flags of the Samajwadi Party fluttering and barge into police stations to beat the cops for having sought to enforce laws. The sight of the police men being beaten in full public views sent the message to the larger population as a wild fire. The people in the state began ruing their decisions to have voted for such an anarchist political party.

Thugs from within the Muslim community and Yadavs would unleash reigns of terror in the state. They had long been in fear of Mayawati and had curbed their instincts. With change in government, they came to their natural selves. The police personnel too saw the iron grip of over them loosening. They dreaded Mayawati. They were extra cautious about lapses on their parts, because Mayawati would be just one phone call away, and they would literally wet their pants. Goons had gone into shells for five years till Mayawati was in power, for they knew she would break their backs. They all joyously returned to reclaim their territories. And they came back with a vengeance.

The scheduled castes, the most backward castes, and the extremely backward castes lived fearless lives in the times of Mayawati government. They constitute over 40 per cent of the population of Uttar Pradesh, and along with the upper castes, including Brahmin, Thakur, Bhumihar and others have potential to form quite a formidable political constituency. Mayawati had commanded absolute majority in the 2007 state elections owing to such a social engineering, which was scripted and executed by her Brahmin mascot Satish Chandra Mishra.

In 2012 people in the state rejected Mayawati not for her lapses on law and order front, but for her excesses in other spheres. She invited ridicule by erecting her own statues in the company of her mentor Kanshi Ram and party symbol elephants. Her image of a queen living lavish life was talk of the town. She was not accessible to any, including her own party workers. She was a monarch. She had tight grip over the law and order. She spearheaded developmental works through townships and roads. But the image was of a monarch living off a lavish life at the expanse of the people. She had peaked politically in 2007 and afterwards she had to slide only on a steep slope. In seven years, she touched the ground after flying high when her party scored a perfect zero in the 2014 elections.

People told Maywati through ballots that democracy and monarchical lifestyle are anti-thesis of each other. They rejected her only to teach her a lesson. Within a year, people regretted their decisions. They would vow to bring back 'Madam' in 2017. But much water would flow into the Ganges in the meantime to make Mayawati out of the schemes of the state politics. She would struggle for limelight post-2014 elections. Days of glory were over. Her 2007 script had run the full course. She has not yet found a new script.

Law and order was collateral damage due to the aloofness of Akhilesh from administration. Not less than 179 communal riots were reported from various parts of Uttar Pradesh in a span of two years since he assumed charge. There were no districts in the state where there had been no cases of communal incidents. The sorry tale of law and order would take ugly turns sometimes later when whole western parts of the state would seethe. Worst communal riots would erupt around Muzaffarnagar in ages.

Mulayam had been in love and hate relationship with Azam. Mulayam had been a political monarch for decades in the state with two mistresses -- Amar Singh and Azam Khan. He could not love both at the same time. His love swung as pendulum from time to time depending upon the political necessities. Mistresses on their parts had their own assets; one had Muslim vote bank, and the other had financial muscles. After Azam flexed his Muslim muscles in 2009 Lok Sabha elections in which Mulayam's dreams of making it big in New Delhi came crashing down, he began flirting with the political 'Nawab' of Rampur one more time. Azam is renowned to have anger on his nose. He has a remarkable ability to lose his temper at any time. He spares none. And he did not spare Akhilesh either. By the time the state headed for 2014 Lok Sabha elections, Azam would ensure that the ruling Samajwadi Party would hit its nadir.

But that will take a while during which Shah would lay down the path for one of the greatest comeback for any political party in the history of the state. The path would be laid so solid, that the BJP would achieve an electoral feat that none could even have dreamt. The feat would ensure safe and sound landing of Modi in New Delhi.

When Lok Sabha elections were just a year away, Shah landed in Lucknow as the state in-charge of the BJP. He carried a specific brief from Modi. The road to power in New Delhi passed through Uttar Pradesh, and he wanted no trespassers.

Shah ensured that by the time people in the state queued up to cast their votes, they just had one name on their leaps -- Narendra Modi. That he could do so was not just because of his infusing life in the party, but by connecting with the people in an extraordinary way, which was not yet seen in Indian politics. Shah would not hold public rallies in those times. He would simply be hopping from one place to another. He would hold meetings after meetings --- all close doors. He would set target with deadlines and follow them up on time. He would not miss any follow up meetings. Party workers would tell about obstacles and he would clear the path in minutes. Party leaders dreaded Shah. But they took prides in Shah also. He put in place a robust party infrastructure right from the booth level to the state headquarters in a matter of a few months. He would know hundreds of party workers at booth levels by names.

By the time Modi began addressing public rallies, crowds in such numbers would gather that rivals would be dwarfed. Make it large was the mantra, and it set off a wind blowing strong enough. Modi wave had begun blowing in Uttar Pradesh. It was not that Uttar Pradesh had not seen 'micro-management' by a political party earlier. Mayawati had scripted such a story in 2007. She had done on the basis of caste engineering under which fragmented groups came together. Shah first looked at polling booths and chose one lakh of them, leaving out 25,000, which were situated in dense Muslim habitations. He was clear that the Muslims would not vote for his party and he would not waste his time seeking them either. He chose six of the best men available in each of these polling booths. They were all provided with smart phones and trained in modern communication skills. These six men in each of one lakh polling booths would later network with people in their respective areas through Facebook, Twitter and WhatsApp. They would emerge as messengers of stories of wonders in which Modi would be the principal hero.

Shah would ensure that his foot-soldiers in polling booths were given enough exposure about development and growth in Gujrat under Modi's stewardship. These foot soldiers were ensured financial muscles and liberty to flex them as they wished. No one asked them how they spent the money. They had direct access to Shah.

The model was replicated at higher levels. Shah would further set up a team of three to four people in each of 74,000 Gram Panchayats. Similar teams were created at block and district levels. Multi-tier teams of people running into hundreds of thousands were in place for revival of the BJP in Uttar Pradesh. In next one year, Shah would continue to hold close-door meetings with such teams and take stock of political changes they were bringing in their respective areas.

When Modi had to address a public rally, Shah's cells from booth to Gram Panchayat, and block to district level would get activated. They will bring people in huge numbers to the venue. They will create buzz days before Modi would address a public meeting. They would spread stories of Gujrat's development and Modi's administrative feats as wildfire in Uttar Pradesh. In the course of one year, many of them went to Gujrat in trains and planes. In Gujrat they saw the way the Gujrat model of development worked. They would select a few people from villages for trips to Gujrat as well. The objective would be to ensure some of the people from each district had been to Gujrat to see 'first hand' what developments had taken place under the leadership of Modi. On their returns, they would talk about their experiences in their villages, and through word of the mouth; stories of Modi's Midas touch would become talk of the town.

The BJP's irony in Uttar Pradesh was of having too many leaders with no limits to their ambitions. Such an irony is cancerous enough to allow growth of any political party. The Congress has slipped into such a quagmire in Madhya Pradesh. Shah's next task was to reign in the state BJP leaders with bloated egos. They were told to specify from where they would like to contest Lok Sabha elections, and that their businesses ended there only. He conveyed that he would not entertain any lobbying for seats from them nor any interference in his works. Within a few months of him assuming the charge of Uttar Pradesh, Shah had bulldozed multitudes of factions within his party. They could not work at cross-purposes as Shah's foot soldiers would drop the word in quick time to him. In 2012 Assembly elections, BJP leaders had worked over time to ensure that candidates of their rivals within the party were defeated.

The Samajwadi Party had joyously reaped collateral benefits of the fratricidal war within the BJP. The incorrigible trouble-makers within the BJP stayed away for fear of consequences if their stories reached the ears of Shah. They dreaded Shah's close doors meetings. Even the gossips ceased within the BJP. Shah could emerge in any town of the state and surprise party leaders and workers with immediate close door meetings. Even senior state level BJP leaders stammered in such meetings, as Shah would demand to know if they had met the challenges, which were set in earlier meetings. Shah would always be on the move. After one year, he would have known each by-lanes of Uttar Pradesh. He was on a mission to ambush rivals. He ended up destroying them.

Azam is senior most ministers in the council of ministers headed by Akhilesh. Along with Mulayam he had founded the Samajwadi Party. Uttar Pradesh has sizable population of Yadavs and Muslims. If these two join together, they can prop up a party of their choice to power. Mulayam knows the importance of Azam. If Muslims desert Samajwadi Party, Mulayam would be just another pedestrian leader. He shrewdly cultivated an image of 'Maulana' Mulayam Singh Yadav to project himself as protector' of Muslims. Later, Mulayam would entertain the idea, that he did not need any Muslim mascot (Azam Khan), because the minority community in the state had no choice but to vote for his party.

His political candour was such that he struck partnership with Kalyan Singh on the eve of the 2009 Lok Sabha elections. Kalyan had been chief minister of Uttar Pradesh and had quit the BJP lately. He is of the Lodh caste, which has sizable population in a few pockets of the state. Amar Singh believed that if Mulayam and Kalyan came together, there could be an envious consolidation of backward caste votes, which can add up with Muslims, 'who had no other choice'. Virendra Bhatiya was a Rajya Sabha MP of the party then and was equally close to Mulayam and Amar Singh. He brought Mulayam and Kalyan together. He would say, 'two leaders can do wonders in the 2009 elections'.

Kalyan was chief minister of the state when the Babri mosque was razed on December 16, 1992. For over a decade he was the target of collective Muslim hatred in the state. Still, Mulayam shook hands with him. Bhatiya would later say that Samajwadi Party could win even 22 Lok Sabha seats in 2009, because Kalyan ensured transfer of Lodh votes. But soon Mulayam would have to publicly disown Kalyan. Bhatiya, who later died of lung infection and was an acclaimed lawyer, would say much before the Liberhan Commission report on demolition of Babri mosque was tabled in Lok Sabha in November 2009 that the time had come to part ways for Mulayam and Kalyan. 'Once the Liberhan Commission report is tabled, the ghost of Babri mosque demolition would come out again and for that matter Mulayam would have to publicly snap ties with Kalyan.' Incidentally, Mulayam and Kalyan had informal arrangements. Soon, Kalyan was dumped in the cold.

Muslims in India perfected the art of tactical voting during the period the BJP made its mark. Muslims would vote with sole objective to ensure defeat of the BJP candidates. Uttar Pradesh, Bihar and West Bengal have seen the impact of tactical voting by Muslims. But they on their own cannot decide the outcome of the elections. They need to add on to other strong caste groups for desired results. Western Uttar Pradesh and West Bengal are somewhat similar in the sense that Muslims are numerically strong, with rough estimates pegging their population at about 25 per cent and more. Locals in western Uttar Pradesh believe that the Muslim population in their areas is much more than 25 per cent and to drive home the point they mention that Rashtriya Lok Dal chief Ajit Singh is no more keen on Harit Pradesh due to change in demography of the region.

Muslims in western Uttar Pradesh for ages have lived in peaceful co-existence with Jat, which is a dominant caste of the region. Dalits are numerically strong in western Uttar Pradesh. Muslims could either add on to Dalits or Jats to elect non-BJP candidates in the region. Mayawati enjoyed electoral advantage, as Dalits-Muslims combination proved to be impregnable for rivals. Western Uttar Pradesh was such a bastion for the BSP that the region always seemed to be in the pocket of Mayawati. Samajwadi Party was almost a persona non grata in the region.

Mulayam wanted Azam to change the political demography of the region. Azam would then embark on the path to fulfill the directions of Mulayam, but would only end up leaving trails of blood in the region.

Ever since coming to power in Lucknow in 2012, Azam let himself loose in the state and lit embers of communal discord wherever he delivered his speeches. He sought to change the character of Muslims from one of a tactical voter in election times to that of a dominant and aggressive community. He wanted Muslims to become like Yadavs. He sought to transform the Muslims into a politically aggressive community in western Uttar Pradesh. He would claim near Ghaziabad, that it was Muslims who sacrificed their lives most in the Kargil war. He sought to communally polarize the Muslims. He also unknowingly set off communal polarization of Hindus. Within hours of Azam making claims on the Kargil war, a list of all those killed would flash in WhatsApp messages to people in the region seeking to set the records right, which would be contrary to what was stated by the Muslim mascot of the Samajwadi party.

By the time Uttar Pradesh headed for 2014 elections, as many as 179 communal incidences were reported from various places in the state. The worst happened in Muzaffarnagar, which is heart of western Uttar Pradesh. Jats and Muslims ambushed each other with exultant bloodletting. They had lived in peaceful co-existence, but were now enemies. People in both the community lost their lives. Akhilesh had no administrative control over the police despite being chief minister of the state for two years. In initial days of simmering communal tension, Azam called the shots.

With no jobs to look for locally, Jats in western Uttar Pradesh go into army in hordes. But talk of the town in the region after communal flare up was that each second Jat youth had an FIR (first information report) registered against him at police station. With an FIR in his name, the Jat youth stared into bleak future, with prospect of employment in the Indian army gone. Jats would unleash such a violence later that Mulayam would have to reign in Azam. But by then the story was over. Jats, Gujjars, and Dalits had just one name on their lips -- Modi. And they all wanted to teach a lesson to Samajwadi Party. The Congress leaders would later privately show videos of Mayawati asking her voters to vote for the BJP.

Mulayam's bid to win over western Uttar Pradesh had turned disastrous. He wanted to win over the western Uttar Pradesh, but ended up losing the whole state. Sometimes politics becomes an agent of blood-letting and much of it was shed in western Uttar Pradesh. Mayawati had by then known designs of Mulayam. She allowed the BJP to reap rich electoral harvest in western Uttar Pradesh.

In a bid to secure political future for her party, Mayawati let go her present advantages and skipped the region at the times of communal flare up as well as when the time would come for election campaign. Message went to Dalits that they had to vote for the BJP in the 2014 elections. Later, the Congress leaders would claim that the BJP and Mayawati had tacit understanding by which latter would transfer Dalit votes to the former for reasons not yet clearly known. One possible reason could be Mayawati's desire to eclipse both Mulayam Singh and Ajit Singh from the political map of western Uttar Pradesh.

Mulayam's political experiment burnt electoral prospect of his party to ashes. Shah seized the opportunity by both the hands. The BJP has an undisputed expertise in cashing in on electoral benefits of simmering communal clashes. The saffron party has in its ranks a battery of saffron robed orators who can give spin to localized incidences.

Yogi Adityanath of Gorakhpur emerged most sought after campaigner for the BJP candidates during election campaign. Shah would ensure that Adityanath had best of choppers at his disposal to fly to any place in the state. Adityanath led the carpet bombing with lethal effect. He heads a Math at Gorakhpur, which has its influence far and wide in the state, including Balrampur, Behraich, and Faizabad. Adityanath would break free of Math's limited influence zone and command strong audiences across the state. His speeches make him look like an angry 'sanyasi'. Mulayam will later advise Adityanath to calm down in Lok Sabha after he delivered a fiery speech when the issue of alleged conversion (Ghar Wapsi) was being debated. 'You're a sanyasi. You should be calm. Why are you so angry,' Mulayam would ask Adityanath forcing upon him a restrained smile.

Mulayam's self-goal in letting Azam run amok in the state with his campaign for an aggressive Muslim campaign helped the cause of Shah a great deal. Modi was already a mascot of development. The communal polarization sealed the fate of all his rivals. The way to power in New Delhi passes through Lucknow and Shah had captured the passage exclusively for his 'saheb'. There was no scope for any trespassers. Shah changed political character of Uttar Pradesh in just one year.

Turning of wheel

DHARMA Chakra Pravartana – The wheel of law is always in motion.

The religion founded after Lord Buddha is not popular in India, but his first sermon is still the guiding light of the Lok Sabha, Lower House of Indian Parliament. Embossed boldly above the seat of the Speaker of the Lok Sabha, Buddha's first sermon delivered at Sarnath is a constant reminder to all, that their actions would be weighed and judged.

Atal Bihari Vajpayee could not believe in 2004 that his government had been voted out of power. In his moments of disbelief, his friend and colleague Sharad Yadav visited him one evening just after the verdict. 'Aap bhi haar gaye (you too lost),' Vajpayee quipped looking at his socialist friend. 'Aapko to maaloom hai hum kyun haare... (you know why did we lose),' replied Yadav. Vajpayee sat down for a chat and tea. He wore the sight of abject dejection. Two concurred that the NDA would not have been voted out if Modi had been punished for 'lapses' during post-Godhra riots in 2002 in Gujrat.

Yadav would later say the country did not re-elect Vajpayee because he had failed to act against Modi. 'People forgot all the good works of Vajpayee, and punished him for (mis)deeds of Modi. Yeh desh Modi ko kabhi PM nahi bana sakta (this country can never make Modi a PM), he would predict. Yadav lost another election a decade later. He lost to one whom he calls a 'goonda (goon)'. Pappu Yadav of Rashtriya Janata Dal handed over him another defeat from Madhepura -- 'Rome of Gope (Yadavs)' -- in Bihar. This time people did not reject the NDA, but chose a political alliance under the leadership of Modi with a mandate not seen for two and a half decades.

Vajpayee is no more in good health conditions. He cannot engage anyone in discussions anymore. But if he along with Yadav chatted on 'why' of the 2014 verdict, they may have corrected themselves for their faulty diagnosis of the 2004 results. They would have concurred, that they were wrong in ignoring the first principle of politics, that nothing is impossible. They were wrong on one more count. People are not prisoners of past events, and they can not only set new trends, but demolish established norms too. One such norm, which had been believed to be true as a gospel's truth, was that the BJP could never get a majority in the Lok Sabha on its own. People of Gujrat did not punished Modi for almost 12 years for 'lapses' for post-Godhra riots. When it came for people of India to make a judgment on Modi, images of the post-Godhra riots did not flash in manners as expected by the New Delhi stereotyped narratives. People did not bother about the claims of the 'butcher of Muslims'.

For over a decade, politicians and media with their bases in New Delhi flogged Modi day and night for their beliefs that he had orchestrated killings of Muslims in Gujrat during post-Godhra riots. But the juggernaut of politics of development crushed two decades of politics of secularism and stereotype flogging of Modi under its wheels. Those who had made their fortunes by herding Muslims were squarely rejected. All the past norms to analyze Indian politics were rejected. Electorates broke free of various dogmas afflicting Indian democracy and delivered a verdict to herald a first majority government after a long time. People handed over keys to India's fate to the man who had been most demonized. The Congress president Sonia Gandhi once called him 'Maut ka saudagar (trader of death)'. Her son Rahul Gandhi branded him a man of Adani (a private group with diversified business interests). In the last year of the Manmohan Singh government, the Congress sought to drag him into snoop gate involving a woman whose calls were tapped and records shared with a magazine, which incidentally was an exclusive destination for all such revelations for one and a half decades and whose head is in jail for more than a year now for allegedly molesting a young female journalist. His star investigative reporter is now a leader of Aam Admi

Party who unsuccessfully fought elections from Delhi.

The snoop gate matter was dragged to such an extent that the Manmohan Singh chaired Union Cabinet approved constitution of a commission of enquiry. The alleged snooping involved Modi, Amit Shah and an anonymous woman, who neither made any complaint and nor was she party to the Central government's move. Television media lapped the issue and took pleasure in drumming it up. Yet, no judge could be found to head the Commission of enquiry constituted by none other than the Union Cabinet. The then Minister for Home Affairs Sushil Kumar Shinde was naive enough to tell the media, that no judge had yet been found to head the Commission.

After the resounding 2014 verdict, which shell-shocked the Congress to such an extent that there had been a vertical split within the party, with one section vowing for Sonia and the other for Rahul, there would be murmurs loud enough to be heard in the Lutyens' zone. The BJP had built up strong campaign against Robert Vadra, who is husband of Priyanka Gandhi and Sonia's son-in-law. Rajsthan went to polls five months before the country headed for the Lok Sabha elections. Rajsthan had been ruled by the Congress and its chief minister Ashok Gehlot had been quite a favourite in the Rahul camp. Same was the case with Bhupinder Singh Hooda, who had been the chief minister of Haryana for a decade. He had survived in chief minister's chair despite strong discontent within the state unit of the party against him because of his access in the Rahul camp. Vadra's land deals in the Congress ruled states of Rajsthan and Haryana had hit national headlines. The BJP vowed to investigate the land deals involving Vadra. Modi ridiculed both 'Yuvraj (prince -- meant for Rahul)' and 'Damaad ji (son-in-law -- meant for Vadra)' during election campaigns for state Assemblies in Rajsthan, Madhya Pradesh, Chhatisgarh and Delhi. The issue was so much in public conscience that they instantly connected to it the moment Modi merely uttered 'Damaad ji'. He did not need to elaborate it.

Vasundhara Raje Scindia of the BJP became the chief minister of Rajsthan five months before the Congress led UPA would be voted out of power at the Centre. She too had centered her election campaign on the alleged unscrupulous land deals involving Vadra in her state. Six months after Modi would be crowned the new prince of Indian politics, Haryana too would go for Assembly elections. Vadra would be an issue on which the BJP would hit the election trails. People would reject the decade long Congress rule in the state headed by Hooda. Manohar Lal Khattar of the BJP who came from the RSS pedigree would be sworn in as chief minister. Yet, no action would be taken against the purported unscrupulous land deals involving Vadra either in Rajsthan or Haryana. Ruling BJP in both the states would conveniently forget their election slogans.

The Congress leaders belonging to Sonia camp would confide that there had been a deal on the snoop gate issue. 'After the loss in the Rajsthan Assembly, the Congress knew the party stood no chance to win the Lok Sabha elections five months later. The deal was brokered in New Delhi with senior BJP leaders for a quid pro quo, which involved inaction on the part of the UPA government on the Commission of enquiry in the snoop gate in exchange for commitment to spare Vadra from any future investigations in his alleged land deals in Rajsthan and Haryana,' said a prominent Congress leader, who had been a party spokesperson before the 2014 verdict. (The Haryana government did constitute an enquiry into all land deals under the previous government. Decision of the state government incidentally came after Rahul, who returned after 57 days of sabbatical, launched frontal personal attack on Modi in Lok Sabha and outside. Much time has gone by and the people are yet to know what were those unscrupulous land deals involving Vadra. By all indications, the wait would be endless.

The Congress leader belonged to that camp in the Congress, which sought to stop Modi's march to 7, Race Course Road (RCR) through judicial means. The Congress thought that the Central Bureau of Investigation (CBI) would nail Modi in various cases. The CBI could not pin Modi down. Amar Singh had famously called the CBI 'a Congress Bureau of Investigation'. And he had named the 'caged bird' for reasons well known in the political circles. The track record of the CBI is not so rosy that it could be written in golden letters. What does it really specialize in is that the cases could go on for generations for their memories to fade away and some of them could stay buried deep in the bed of inaction, while some would buzz with life as per the whims and fancies of the ruling dispensation at the Centre. The Congress' excessive obsession with Modi from the times when he was not yet on the radar of national politics enlarged his profile to such levels in later years that he literally eclipsed the grand old party. The Congress had played a major part in building the profile of Modi large enough for him to seek a national role. The Congress' hatred for Modi had been to such an extent that Jairam Ramesh, who was a Union Minister in the Manmohan Singh Cabinet, would write a letter to him every month, but address him just as 'Shri Narendra Modi' against his practice of prefixing 'Dear', 'My Dearest', etc., for other chief ministers. The hatred was personal and not political. And the hatred was on account of morbid fear.

Each year before the annual plan meeting, members of the Planning Commission would be briefed by the Congress leaders to grill Modi on social indicators when he visited Yojna Bhavan. Sayeeda Hameed of the Planning Commission would dig out figures to corner Modi on status of malnourishment, infant and maternal mortality rates and so on in Gujrat. The Planning Commission was turned into a political body to go after Modi, with data and statistics on poor performance of Gujrat on social indicators fed to the media to counter the claims of the development model being sought at that time worthy for replication across the country. The Congress hammered the last nail in the coffin of the Planning Commission by exploiting it for political purposes. One of the very first acts of Modi after being sworn in as Prime Minister was to shut it down. He would unveil a NITI (National Institution for Transforming India) Aayog, which would rather be a brainstorming body to evolve solutions for issues affecting governance wherein the powers would be vested in chief ministers and not those retired bureaucrats.

Five months before the 2014 Lok Sabha elections, a critical electoral battle was fought in Chhatisgarh, which had been bleeding with Maoist onslaught for years. Chhatisgarh went to the polls along with Rajsthan, Madhya Pradesh, and Delhi. Modi pulled unprecedented crowd in Rajsthan and Madhya Pradesh, but Chhatisgarh along with Delhi were tough battles. The maverick Ajit Jogi of the Congress still was a fox keeping rivals on the toes. He commanded strong support in Chattisgarh despite being wheel-chair bound. Modi would pour his all energy in Chhatisgarh to beat the anti-incumbency against the BJP's Raman Singh led government. The Congress leaders with much glee would tell that they were told by the New Delhi caucus within the BJP that Modi had been made to address even street corner public meetings in Chhatisgarh, and a defeat there would directly be read as vote against him. The Chhatisgarh battle went to the wires, and the BJP scraped through narrowly. This feat of Modi established him as the sole flag-bearer of the BJP, and the 2014 Lok Sabha elections would later turn out to be just about him. If not for Modi, the Congress would have staged a comeback in Chhatisgarh after a decade of the BJP rule. But the Modi wave had set in and taken Chhatisgarh in its full grip. The BJP registered massive electoral wins in Madhya Pradesh and Rajsthan. The wins were of such scales that the Congress workers were too demoralized to put up fight five months later in the Lok Sabha elections. It also emerged that if not for Modi, the NGO politician Arvind Kejriwal would have formed a government with full majority in Delhi.

The BJP's highest tally in Lok Sabha was 182 in 1998. A year later when the country voted Vajpayee back into power the tally did not go up or down and stayed at 182. The previous best performance for the BJP was in 1996 when the country voted out the Congress led government under P V Narsimha Rao. The BJP had won 161 Lok Sabha seats. The saffron party had 120 seats in 1991, while in 1989 BJP had won 85 Lok Sabha seats when the country voted out the Rajiv Gandhi government after the Bofors taint. Viswanath Pratap Singh had walked out of the Rajiv Gandhi government to hit the roads with the slogan of 'ye jo gaal ki laali hai, Bofors ki dalaali haai (rosy cheeks are on account of Bofors kickbaks)'. In the 1984 elections, the BJP had a unique feat of winning just two seats. From 1984 to 1999, the BJP graph kept rising and afterwards sank to 138 in the 2004 Lok Sabha elections and went further down to 116 in 2009. The 1999 was the peak of the BJP and acted as the ceiling for the party. Even political pundits and the New Delhi caucus within the BJP believed that the party was not capable of scaling the wall of 182 seats because of the geographical handicap. The BJP was a party of the North, Central and western parts of India. The BJP seemed to have not enough footprints in eastern and southern parts of India to become the Congress of its golden days. The best guess of political pundits would be about 220 Lok Sabha seats for the BJP.

India could not think beyond the handicap of coalition politics, as if it had become a fate with which nothing could have been done. People proved the political pundits utterly wrong. The BJP won the 2014 by huge margin. Modi powered the BJP to break the psychological barrier of 182 to zoom to 282 Lok Sabha seats, which was an additional century to the previous peak. The halfway mark in the Lok Sabha is 272 in the House of 543 to form a government. The BJP led pre-poll political alliance of the NDA got 336 Lok Sabha seats. The 2014 mandate drew an immediate parallel with the last single party full majority government of Rajiv in 1984. But it was much more, because Rajiv had not earned the 1984 mandate. People out of sympathy for Indira Gandhi gave her son keys to the fate of India on a platter. India had not yet known abilities of Rajiv. In contrast, the 2014 mandate was earned by Modi, with people investing in him for his works as a chief minister of Gujrat for about 12 years. The 2014 mandate could not be compared even with the massive Indira win in 1980 for the reason that the people voted her back into power after getting fed up with the pedestrian and fratricidal Janata experiment of 1977 and with the belief that only the Congress could rule the country.

The 2014 mandate was largely a positive mandate for development of India as promised by Modi. It was for nation building and, hence, the 1957 mandate won by Pandit Jawahar Lal Nehru fits best for a comparison. India sought to repose its faith again in a strong leadership, who promised industrialization. People rejected the status quo ways of the Congress along with its povertarian ideologies. The Congress' core campaign built on secularism and anti-poverty policies, which were embedded into Indian politics by Indira, found no takers in 2014. India voted for a politically strong Prime Minister. Five years after Advani had sought to tell people of the consequences of a weak Prime Minister, people understood the meaning when the full scale of pitfalls were known to them through various revelations made by the Comptroller and Auditor General (CAG). The mandate was against the dual power centres as had been the case during the decade long UPA rule. And, most importantly, people unyoked themselves from emotional bondage to the Congress. People rallied behind the BJP as a credible alternative to the Congress. The verdict gave a morbid blow to the belief that the Congress was the most powerful pole of Indian politics. The space had been surrendered.

The Congress slumped to a humiliating figure of 44 Lok Sabha seats. The party made history by staying in double digits, and further improved its previous worst performance of 1999 Lok Sabha elections when the party had won 114 seats. The Congress got just seven seats more than the AIADMK, which won all its 37 seats from just one state Tamil Nadu. The Congress' 44 came from across the country and largely from the North-east, Karnatka and Kerala. The Congress surely did not look like a national party. The party had hit its nadir when the Congress fought Lok Sabha elections for the first time under Rahul's leadership. His political baptism had largely been in the states of Uttar Pradesh and Maharashtra. He had been staying in Dalit hamlets in these two states. India at large did not much of him. Rahul would seek to ambush his political opponents by appearing at dawn riding a motorcycle in Bhatta Parsaul in western Uttar Pradesh to throw his weight behind farmers agitating claims of forced land acquisition. For over two years, Rahul's politics would revolve around the issue of land acquisition and would prevail upon the UPA government to enact a law, which would be opposed by even the Congress government in Maharashtra. Under Rahul, the Congress approached the 2014 battle with a bouquet of entitlement based laws, which included the National Food Security Act.

Rahul presented people with a bouquet of entitlement based laws when they aspired for jobs. He hit the campaign trails with an anti-industry image. He had sought to ambush the setting up of industries in Odisha by seeking to champion the cause of tribals. His party did not open an account in Odisha in the 2014 Lok Sabha elections. Uttar Pradesh was his political nursery, but the rejected his party comprehensively. Only consolation for the Congress in Uttar Pradesh was that the mother-son duo (Sonia and Rahul) retained their Rae Bareli and Amethi constituencies respectively. But Rahul had his share of sleepless nights when the BJP's Smirti Irani scared him enough by putting up spirited fight by coming close enough to brighten the prospect of a major electoral upset. If Samajwadi Party had put up a candidate against Rahul, his fate would have been sealed. Even after losing elections in Amethi, Irani would emerge as a star in the Modi cabinet and would continue to challenge the Gandhi family scion in his pocket-borough.

Not only for the Gandhi dynasty but other political family enterprises which had cropped in the previous three decades faced mortal blow from

Modi. Mulayam and Ajit Singh had formed family owned political enterprises in Uttar Pradesh. Lalu Prasad and Om Prakash Choutala had similar ones in Bihar and Haryana respectively. Mulayam's Samajwadi Party was routed. His party won only five Lok Sabha seats, and, incidentally, all of them were from his clan. Mulayam's nephews -- Dharmendra Yadav, Akshay Yadav and Tej Pratap Yadav, besides daughter-in-law Dimple Yadav -- are members of Lok Sabha from Samajwadi Party. The clan members could win because the Akhilesh Yadav's led state government had mobilized whole state government machinery to ensure their wins. In two years times, Samajwadi Party after gaining absolute majority in the state Assembly slumped to a strength of a mere five seats out of the total 80 from the kitty of India's largest state. Mulayam's dream of becoming Prime Minister turned into a nightmare. Choudhary Charan Singh's legacy was exploited by his son Ajit Singh to found another family owned political enterprise in western Uttar Pradesh. Rashtriya Lok Dal of Ajit Singh was blown away in the Modi wave. His son Jayant Choudhary lost to the BJP's Hema Malini from Mathura Lok Sabha seat. The father-son duo treated the western Uttar Pradesh as their fiefdom. After one of the public meeting in Shamli when they flew away to New Delhi in a chopper, local Jats would say 'Dilli ud gawo baap beto (they have flown away to Delhi)' quite sarcastically to suggest their disconnect with people on the ground. Ajit Singh was defeated from his family pocket-borough Baghpat by Satyapal Singh of the BJP, who had just joined politics after quitting job in the police.

In Haryana, Om Prakash Choutala had carried forward legacy of Choudhary Devi Lal through his family owned political enterprise Indian National Lok Dal (INLD). He knew that Haryana was in the grip of the Modi wave. Accordingly, he made it a point to tell people that after the elections his party would support Modi in forming a government at the Centre even though his party was not in a pre-poll alliance of the NDA. People in Haryana did not fall for his trap and opted for direct connections with Modi. The INLD was routed, with the party drawing solace with just two seats. The consolation for ageing Choutala was his grandson Dushyant Choutala winning the poll.

Lalu went into the 2014 Lok Sabha elections quite handicapped. He was convicted and debarred from contesting elections. His family owned political enterprise nonetheless fielded his wife Rabri Devi from Saran and daughter Misa Yadav from Patna City Lok Sabha seats. By the time people cast their votes, Misa had collected so much of saris that she had no place to keep them. Wherever she went in the constituency, people feted Misa as their own daughter. Lalu had lost from the same Lok Sabha seat in the 2004 elections. He knew the electoral battle for his daughter was tough. He pulled all tricks up his sleeves to ensure safe sailing for his daughter. His long time loyalist Ram Kripal Yadav had walked into the BJP camp and was the candidate against his daughter. Patna city constituency has sizable population of both Yadavs and Bhumihars. Lalu thought of splitting the Bhumihar votes. Brahmeshwar Mukhiya was a venerable figure for Bhumihars. He had founded Ranbir Sena to fight the rise of Maoists in neighbouring districts of Bhojpur. During the times of Lalu and Rabri Devi as chief ministers of Bihar, Mukhiya had enjoyed the state patronage in clandestine manners. It was only after the ouster of Lalu from seat of power that Mukhiya was gunned down in broad daylight. Mukhiya's family owed a debt to Lalu for his favours in tough times when Ranbir Sena chief was hounded by judiciary and police. With his death, the curtain also came down on Ranbir Sena.

But Maosits were again rearing their heads in Bhojpur region. Mukhiya's son Indu Bhushan sought to reclaim legacy of his father and wanted to try his luck in politics. Lalu called him up to contest the 2014 Lok Sabha elections from Patna city as an Independent. The trick was that he would cut into Bhumihar votes, and, thus, help Misa win her maiden elections to Indian Parliament. The plan was executed. But Modi wave was too strong for such tricks. Misa lost and so did her mother from Saran. The RJD could win only four Lok Sabha seats in Bihar out of the total 40 seats. Lalu's charisma was history.

The 2014 mandate was against family owned political enterprises, which were deeply etched in states of Uttar Pradesh, Bihar and Haryana. West Bengal, Odisha and Tamil Nadu ducked the Modi wave. The BJP did not have infrastructure in these states to translate good-wills of people into votes. In West Bengal, Mamata Banerjee led Trinamool Congress had just come to power three years ago after uprooting 34 years long reign of the Left parties. The BJP won two seats in West Bengal, but the state backed Banerjee. Her party along with Biju Janata Dal and AIADMK are not family owned political enterprises, but individual centric on the lines of the Mayawati led Bahujan Samajwadi Party. In Odisha, Navin Patnaik led BJD enjoys popular support base. His party is blessed with remarkable and energetic leaders who stay connected with people. The BJD is the only political party, which as a matter of rule, never troops into well of the House in Parliament. Its members in Lok Sabha and Rajya Sabha make well researched and strongly argued speeches. The Trinamool Congress, the BJD, and the AIADMK swept the 2014 Lok Sabha elections with near 100 per cent strike rates, while ceding a few seats to the BJP. The Congress was wiped out in Odisha and Tamil Nadu, while the party could win just two seats in West Bengal. These three parties along with Telangana Rashtra Samithi and Telaghu Desham Party in Andhra Pradesh (a pre-poll alliance partner of the BJP) emerged unscathed from the Modi wave.

Otherwise, the Modi wave blew strongly in whole of Western, Northern, Central and eastern parts of the country, taking into its ambit even Assam. The BJP registered near 100 per cent strike rate in Gujrat, Rajsthan, Maharashtra, Haryana, Uttar Pradesh, Madhya Pradesh, Delhi, Himachal Pradesh, Jharkhand, while winning substantial number of seats in Bihar, Chhatisgarh, Karnatka and Punjab. The wave covered even the northern most state of Jammu and Kashmir. A few months later, the BJP would make history by becoming part of the state government in the state through a curious alliance with People's Democratic Party (PDP) led by Mufti Mohammed Sayeed, who had been much closer to Janata parties, besides being Minister for Home Affairs in the VP Singh government at the Centre. The wave had enough leg for another six months of run to allow the BJP to come to power in Haryana, Maharashtra, and Jharkhand. The BJP would be so confident of the Modi wave that the party would unyoke ties with the Shiv Sena and go solo in the state elections. Only after missing the half way mark with a whisker, the BJP would embrace Shiv Sena back, but on its own terms.

The power of Modi persona would be such that he would give Haryana a non-Jat chief minister in Manohar Lal Khattar. He would opt for a non-tribal Raghubar Das in Jharkhand. In Maharashtra, he would defy the stereotype and choose a Brahmin chief minister in Devendra Fadnavis. All three were unlikely contenders for the posts of chief ministers in their respective states and carried no past baggage. They can think fresh and could bring new ideas on the table. Even during the campaign for the Lok Sabha elections, the BJP chief Rajnath Singh would ask scribes of what they had seen on the ground during their field reporting and when told that people were not voting for his party but for Modi he would nod in acknowledgement. 'I know people are voting for Modi ji only.'

The 2014 Lok Sabha elections were all about Modi. The BJD's Lok Sabha leader Bhartruhari Mahtab would later explain how the Modi wave was stopped in Odisha. 'We told people Modi is from Gujrat, and we are going to stay with you being so near to you. People were at ease to relate with us. They could not relate to a Gujrati,' he would say. But Odisha along with Tamil Nadu were exceptions in an otherwise Modi show. West Bengal will see hope in Modi for the BJP to become a challenger to Mamata Banerjee. Even though the BJP would scale down attack on her in bargain for tacit support in the Parliament for passage of the key reform measures, Banerjee would begin weighing the option to advance state Assembly elections to ward off threat from the saffron party. The 2014 mandate marked a decisive break from the Indian political history. In the 1960s, anti-Congressism took a few baby steps. The advent of Indira on the political scene nourished politics of anti-Congressism. Her excesses galvanized the politics of anti-Congressism in the 1970s. India's second generation of Indian politicians owe their political baptism to their 19 months long jail terms during the Emergency imposed by Indira. India saw the mother-son duo of Indira and Sanjay Gandhi wreaking havoc with the country. The destructive streak of Sanjay's, which was ably nourished by his ruffian friend circle that had envious access to the corridors of power, left trails of human and social agonies for the country to account for decades to come.

It was in that time that Indian bureaucracy metamorphosed into a political parasite and institutionalized sycophancy for political class. Those who were in bureaucracy and were classmates of Sanjay Gandhi or known to him somehow would humiliate their seniors and exercise disproportionate power. One of them was NK Singh or 'Nandu'. He was joint secretary rank officer in New Delhi. But the near capitulation of bureaucracy to Sanjay Gandhi's whims and fancies saw NK Singh emerging a powerful bureaucrat. He had been a classmate of Sanjay Gandhi. A journalist recalled that once he was sitting across NK Singh in his office and his superior, who was a secretary, walked in to say a few words to him. 'He waved to suggest he was busy talking to him and made him wait in his room without even offering a chair to seat. We were having no serious discussion and I wanted to leave, but was made to stay. He prolonged the chit-chat, while his superior kept waiting and standing. He just wanted to humiliate the secretary, who was also seeking some favour from Sanjay Gandhi through him,' the journalist would recall, while speaking of Sanjay Gandhi days. This bureaucrat would emerge as a politician with connections in all the parties in later decades.

For next four decades anti-Congressism would be the cornerstone of Indian politics. So much so that the Left and Right of Indian politics would prop up the National Front government of VP Singh in 1989 in their singular bid to keep Congress out of power. The politics of anti-Congressism would spread far and wide, with a number of regional parties firming up their bases in their respective regions. Congress would slump to about 140 Lok Sabha seats in the 1996 and 1998 Lok Sabha elections. The party would further nosedive in 1999 only to stage a comeback after a combative Sonia Gandhi took charge of the party.

The mother-son duo of Indira and Sanjay had galvanized India's second generation of leaders in the non-Congress space, which included Jayaprakash Narayan, Ram Manohar Lohiya, Atal Bihari Vajpayee, Choudhary Charan Singh, Devi Lal, George Fernandes, LK Advani, Sharad Yadav, Mulayam Singh Yadav among others. India's third generation of leaders, which would include Narendra Modi, Nitish Kumar, Mamata Banerjee, Naveen Patnaik, Rajnath Singh and others, would take the centre stage during the decade when the mother-son duo of Sonia Gandhi and Rahul Gandhi called the shots in the corridors of power. But this decade will not lead to further wave of anti-Congressism. In place, the Congress would become friendly to a large number of regional and small parties. The Congress would cease to be a threat to them and a larger foe in the form of BJP would loom large posing existential threat to them. They will publicly claim that the era of anti-Congressism is over. 'The era of anti-Congressism is now over. Now, it's time for all to unite against the BJP,' Sharad Yadav would say in the aftermath of the 2014 verdict.

The BJP had dropped a strong anchor in the Indian politics. The 2014 mandate dawned political stability not seen for many decades. It gave a decisive slap to those who sought to bleed India by exploiting political instability for their gains. Cynicism and negativism made hasty retreats following the mandate. The Modi era had begun. A politically strong leader with extraordinary skill to communicate with the people occupied the 7, Race Course Road. Politics in India would now be Modi versus others. But there would be none with stature of him in the immediate horizon to give face to the Opposition.

Modi had dream-walked the muddied waters.

Brazen bursts

INAUGURATION of Narendra Modi as India's Prime Minister on May 26, 2014 was on a bold note.

He defied stereotypes and invited all leaders of the South Asian nations. His inauguration was an event of an unprecedented scale on its own, yet he invited Pakistan premier Nawaz Sharif.

Modi had been an acerbic critic of India's even subtle gestures to improve relations with Pakistan. The BJP's mentor, Rashtriya Swayam Sevak Sangh (RSS), has a fixed historical narrative in which Pakistan is branded an illegitimate child of the policies of Muslim appeasement of the Congress practiced during pre-Independence days. Modi showed his bold streak to defy possible backlash from the saffron camps and invited Sharif on his inauguration to the majestic forecourt of the Rashtrapati Bhavan on the Raisina Hills.

Manmohan Singh in his decade long premiership shunned India's neighbours except for Bangladesh and Bhutan. He would stay off from Pakistan, Sri Lanka and Nepal. India's relations with these three South

Asian nations would only head south. The UPA did not disturb status quo in India's relations with her immediate neighbours. Policy of detachment with South Asian neighbours would soon have China right there on India's doors. The overwhelming political flavor in Nepal had been to befriend China. Sri Lanka under Mahinda Rajpaksha, who ruled the island nation from 2005 till 2015, sought to give China a firm landing much to the discomfort of New Delhi. The tiny island nation of Maldives on a regular basis pricked Indian ego, with the old maverick Abdul Gayoom playing tricks in upstaging pro-India leader Mohammed Nasheed. Pakistan stayed stuck in its self-made web of deaths and destruction. India was tired of an incorrigible Pakistan, which played dangerous game of terror and politics, with spillover effects in her neighbours.

Even before Modi took oath of the office, he called for India's change of approach towards South Asian neighbours. He would later unveil the policy of pro-active engagement. Under Sheikh Hasina, Bangladesh had been reigning in rabid anti-India Islamists. She delivered on India's demands to reign in fugitive militants of Assam and the other North-east states. Manmohan Singh's only diplomatic success in the immediate neighbourhood was improvement in the ties with Bangladesh. He ensured a benign credit extension of $ one billion to Dhaka allow funding of infrastructure development in Bangladesh, while substantially diluting custom duties for imports. All that Hasina wanted from the Manmohan Singh government was ratification of pact on land boundary and Teesta river water sharing. Singh was keen to deliver on the twin promises, but he was policy paralysed to move even an inch forward. India disappointed Hasina. Indeed, India needs Bangladesh to bring her North-eastern states closer to the mainland. She, however, had a feel of the wind blowing in India, and, accordingly, sent her emissary to Ahmedabad to meet Modi. He obviously reassured the emissary. Modi delivered on the land boundary pact before his government completed first anniversary in the office. Indian Parliament approved the Constitution amendment proposal to resolve a legacy of India's brutal partition. Freedom finally came for scores of people stuck in no man's land. Modi further needs to deliver on sharing of Teesta river waters. Bangladesh being a lower riparian nation desires water security.

Maithripala Sirisena did a world of good for India by dethroning Mahinda Rajapaksha in Sri Lanka. Rajapaksha had been warming up to China, while denying legitimate rights of Tamilians in northern region of the island. India's 'deep assets' proved useful in mobilizing a united Opposition against Rajpaksha before the island nation went for the polls (2015). Sirisena is expected to undo the Rajpaksha damages to both the Indian and Tamilian interests in the coming years.

Modi infused life in India's moribund relations with Nepal. He made a remarkable bold statement in his address to Nepalese Parliament that they could tear off the historical pact with India and script a new one of their liking. Nepal's relations with India were such that the Himalayan country did not bother to appoint an ambassador in New Delhi for three years (2012-15). Indian response following the massive Nepal earthquake was remarkable eliciting global applause. Modi took the lead to reach rescue teams to the Himalayan nation. If not for stupid reportage of Indian television media obsessed with jingoism, India may have scripted a turnaround in the hearts of Nepalese. India's multitude of woes, including the menace of Maoist violence and dumping of counterfeit currency, demand proactive action on the part of Nepal to turn their taps off. Modi took bold measures in India's immediate neighbourhood to secure and safeguard the national interest, which will pay dividends subsequently.

No great nation is ring-faced with hostile nations. But India had been in such a trap for decades, with strategists in New Delhi leaving monstrous challenges for posterity by their obsession with status quo.

The BJP has an emotional attachment with Jammu and Kashmir. The party founder Shyama Prasad Mukherjee had challenged the combined might of Pandit Jawahar Lal Nehru and Sheikh Abdullah on special status to the state given in the form of Article 370 of India's Constitution. The BJP and Rashtriya Swayamsevak Sangh (RSS) glorify Ballabh Bhai Patel (Sardar Patel) and demonize Nehru, because of the way the first government in the Independent India handled the issue of Kashmir. If Nehru had been more nationalist and a little less internationalist, not an inch of the Kashmir valley would have been in the possession of Pakistan. If Patel had handled accession of the princely state of Jammu and Kashmir, the course of history arguably may have been different. History is intriguing, because it's dotted with too many 'ifs'. The RSS is fascinated with those historical 'ifs' and 'buts'.

Jammu and Kashmir is one state only for a namesake. People of Jammu despise disproportionate attention to the Kashmir valley. Those in Laddakh seldom figure on the radar of those who matter and sometimes blip only when there happens to be a few incursions by the adventurous Chinese army. The Congress for decades enjoyed popular support in Jammu, while National Conference somehow managed to win elections in the Kashmir valley. The state of status quo prevailed over the state for decades under the National Conference and the Congress regime. The youth in the valley grew up in the times of militancy and have seen excesses of the security forces. A section of the Kashmiri youth despise India and seek to identify with Pakistan. A few minutes of conversations with a Kashmiri youth would easily give out their psyche. The Kashmiri youth call separatist Hurriyat Conference leader Syed Ali Shah Geelani a Mahatma Gandhi of the valley. Indeed, New Delhi and Srinagar have a lot of distance to bridge. But Modi's arrival on the national scene disturbed the fine balance prevailing in the state. The new man in New Delhi came with an image that he had no stomach for the status quo.

The BJP swept the Jammu region, and the People's Democratic Party (PDP) and National Conference won seats in the Kashmir valley in state elections after a few months of the inauguration of Modi in New Delhi. The Congress lost its plot in the state. The mandate was obviously for an alliance of the BJP and PDP, who were poles apart in their political attitudes. The PDP leader Mufti Mohammed Sayeed is a socialist with roots in anti-Congress politics. He seeks to heal wounds of the people in the valley. The BJP seeks firm integration of the state with the rest of India.

Militancy in late 1980s and 1990s in the state ethnically cleansed the valley of its Pundit population. The National Conference and Congress regime in the state showed tokenism on the issue of rehabilitation of Pundits. People with roots in the valley for ages became refugees in their own country. Ironically, Kashmiri pundits have been treated worse than even the German Jews. They were ethnically cleansed and their properties confiscated or taken away by showing fear of death. No government in New Delhi in the last 25 years showed even an ounce of empathy for the Kashmiri pundits. New Delhi's wonder boy Omar Abdullah would brush away the plight of the Kashmiri pundits, saying Muslims too suffered in the valley in loss of lives. Proponents of status quo surely have an incorrigible habit of arguing in circle.

Advent of Modi on the national scene nudged the BJP and PDP, which are not apologetic about their beliefs and do not shy away from expressing them openly, to form a government in Jammu and Kashmir. Modi is equally not shy to assert his views on the issue of Kashmir. He renewed the promises of Atal Bihari Vajpayee made to the people of Kashmir that solutions would be found within the limits of Insaaniyat (humanism). He left the debate on Article 370 open-ended. But Modi was different from his predecessors in allowing the rituals of Pakistan meddling in the affairs of Kashmir by feting Hurriyat leaders in her embassy in the Chanakyapuri area in New Delhi. Modi has shown that he's touchy about such Pakistani overt indulgences in the affairs of Kashmir. Modi's inauguration happened in the presence of Nawaz Sharif. Two of them decided to resume Foreign Secretary level engagements. But the moment Pakistani ambassador in New Delhi as a matter of habit hosted leaders of Hurriyat on the eve of the resumption of the formal diplomatic exchange, Modi brought the curtain down. Pakistan will have to mind its business if she wants to resume formal talks with

India. Modi demonstrated at least on two occasions that he cared least for dimplomatic niceties and Pakistan would have to know that the old narrative of relations between the two nations have run the full course. Modi wants Pakistan to act more on terror than show occasional concerns for Kashmir.

In April, 2015, Chinese President Xi Jinping visited Pakistan and pledged an investment of $46 billion to build highways and dams in Pakistan Occupied Kashmir, which would to eventually connect with a transnational highway connecting Gowdar port in the Baloochistan province to the Chinese mainland. This happened a month before Modi embarked on his maiden official visit to China. But a day before he embarked on his flight for X'ian province in China, which is also the hometown of Jinping, media was told that India had strongly asked Beijing to stay away from Pakistan Occupied Kashmir. In X'ian, Modi told Jinping that Pakistan Occupied Kashmir is not a playground for China and he should stay away from the region. In September 2014 when Jinping was in New Delhi, a small unit of People's Liberation Army of China was perched in Chunar valley of Laddakh as part of their regular intrusions. Modi gathered data of all such incursions, including those which took place at the times of visits by heads of the states of the two countries, and confronted Jinping, asking if Chinese army wanted to damage the relations. Adventurism on Indo-China border since then has pauses.

Modi poses serious challenge to the status quo in the state of Jammu and Kashmir. Nothing happens immediately in his scheme of things, but script for a new narrative on the Himalayan state is already being written in his office.

In less than three months after his inauguration, Modi brought curtain on India's obsession to think about her economy with an old Soviet mindset. He shut down Planning Commission. He brought down the curtain on the Soviet era relic from the ramparts of the Red Fort in a subtle message that the Indian economy was being freed from the clutches of a few retired babus. For more than six decades, babus perched in air-conditioned rooms in New Delhi decided what state governments should do, because of compulsive belief that the socio-economic intellectual capital was vested in the national capital only. That the Planning Commission survived even the collapse of the Soviet Union reflects deep roots of the New Delhi caucus in the Indian statecraft.

New Delhi is a unique place, besides being the national capital. Bureaucrats never want to leave the city. Policy lobbyists thrive in New Delhi. Non-Governmental Organisations (NGOs) dot the national capital in numbers defying laws of the business. New Delhi is a Mecca of crossover middlemen with knack to get deals done through their connections across the political class, bureaucracy, and the business world. Planning Commission was the high temple of the New Delhi caucus. The Planning Commission was also akin to a bully monitor in a classroom where Prime Minister played the role of a principal and state governments were like students. It resisted too many changes and its members were arguably blessed with stereotyped mindsets.

When Sheila Dikshit was still chief minister of the National Capital Territory of Delhi (2007), she thought of doings things different in the public distribution system (PDS) through which over $15 billion of food subsidy is annually pumped in the country. She told the Planning Commission in an annual Plan meeting that she wanted to take up a pilot project to give cash in place of foodgrains under PDS. Sayeeda Hameed of the Planning Commission kept lecturing Dikshit in that meeting, 'you give cash, the poor will consumer liquor, and their children will go hungry'. Dikshit was concerned, because the poor were not getting even the grains, as they were diverted to the black market. Planning Commission in its own report had noted a few years ago, that up to 48 per cent of the grains under PDS end up in the black market. This vicious circle of organized loot in the name of food subsidy has survived all modern changes.

Modi to his credit ended the lordship of the Planning Commission. Additionally, he agreed to the 14th Finance Commission report for devolution of 42 per cent of Central taxes to state governments, which had earlier been 32 per cent. Two measures taken together would end the practice of the Central government making all kinds of schemes for states, which logically and prudently should have been local concerns.

'Humne hazaaron karor rupye Dilli se bheja, leking Lucknow me jo Haathi hai wo paisa khata hai ... (We send thousands of corores of rupees, but the elephant in Lucknow devour them...),' Rahul Gandhi would say in a public meeting in Saharanpur in Uttar Pradesh in 2012, with senior Congress leader Digvijay Singh gleefully indulging in his passion of photography on the stage. The Gandhi scion would say the same things even in 2010 in Bihar. He would still say the same things to people in 2014. He said so because his father Rajiv Gandhi too had spoken the same words. He had said about two and a half decades back, that only 15 paise out of one rupee that New Delhi sends to states reaches people. In the span of 25 pears, there was a 'monumental' correction in Gandhi's statement, as last Deputy Chairman of Planning Commission Montek Singh Ahluwalia said in 2014 that 'the amount is actually now 16 paisa'. New Delhi thought as a landlord.

Besides bold interventions, Modi showed his brazen streak.

Jantar Mantar is a bylane at a stone's throw from the Parliament. A walk through the Jantar Mantar on any day may help one to gauge the pulse of India's vibrant democracy. On one such leisure walk, a woman's angry utterances were heard from a long distance, which gave no sense of what was being said and about the identity of the source of the sound. After a few steps ahead, the booming noise turned little coherent. A little more steps and the target of the verbal barrage appeared in the sight. He was a young and small built man in a typical attire, which in New Delhi is known for those who make Jawaharlal Nehru University their permanent stay. He was being led away by Renuka Choudhary. She was a Union minister in the Manmohan Singh Cabinet of UPA-II and also a Congress spokesperson.

She was taking part in an open air debate hosted by a news channel on the issue of proposed 'bifurcation' of Andhra Pradesh (2013). The young man was in the audience and he had asked another participant in the debate. 'If your party favours small states, then why not first bifurcate Gujrat before doing the same with Andhra Pradesh,' he had asked, while adding further: 'Your party supports division of Andhra Pradesh, Will your leader, Narendra Modi, support division of Gujrat, since your party favours smaller states.' The questions brought the open air debate to an abrupt end.

The other woman panelist was from the BJP. She fumed at the question. She leaped at the questioner. Her anger alarmed her co-panelist. Choudhary put her arm on the shoulder of the young man and led him away from the sight of the fuming BJP woman leader. Long after he was out of the sight, she yelled at top of her lung to answer his questions. When he was far off to hear anything what she said, the BJP woman leader shed her residual anger at the escort personnel of the television channel. She left the place with escort's car shaking with anger. Peace finally returned to Jantar Mantar that evening, with leisure walkers getting to hear chirping of birds perched on mighty trees. The BJP woman leader on the stage was Nirmala Sitharaman. She was a spokesperson of the BJP. She is a woman with tight upper lip and plastic facial expression. She was among the BJP spokespersons who spiritedly and stoutly defended Modi when the Congress and other parties sought to hit him below the belt.

On May 26, she was sworn in as Minister of State in the Modi Cabinet and given Independent charge of crucial Commerce portfolio, besides the Finance ministry as a junior minister of Arun Jaitely.

Shrillness in television studios was at the peak during the last three years of UPA-II. They were lynching the UPA ministers on a daily basis.

Every evening they will throw open their kangaroo courts where instant judgment would be delivered. The Congress would be so battered in such television 'discussion' that later no known faces would come to these studios, and in place would come a new crop that hardly had anything to do with politics. Modi would also be a target of such television 'discussions' until they realized that the man was all set to become the Prime Minister following which they transformed from kangaroo courts to courtiers ready to bend their backs beyond possible human limits.

The BJP had two of its leaders who were regular to such studios. They were Piyush Goyal and Smirti Zubin Irani. Goyal would be such a combative television panelist that he would win the game of shouting and running down co-panelists with much ease. His hard work in television studios did not go in vain and he was sworn in as Minister of State with Independent charge in the Modi Cabinet and given critical portfolios of power and coal. Irani overshadowed her two other combative spokespersons and was sworn in as Cabinet Minister with the key portfolio of Human Resources Development. She had among her predecessors Kapil Sibbal, Murali Manohar Joshi, Arjun Singh. Some wanted to know her educational qualifications. She knew she had made raised eyebrows and consequently would shut herself from the glare of the media.

Modi had set twin criteria for becoming ministers. One should not be a son or daughter of a politician still active in politics and he or she should be less than 70 years of age. The BJP's Rajsthan strong woman Vasundhara Raje Scindia sought induction of her son Dushyant Singh in the Cabinet. But he seemed ineligible for obvious reason. In protest she made it a point that Rajsthan went unrepresented in the Cabinet barring one who was not from her camp and he would soon face rape charges. Goyal is in politics because of his father Ved Prakash Goyal, who was a minister in the Council of Ministers headed by Atal Bihari Vajpayee. For Modi, political dynasty meant two generations being active in politics at the same time, and he surely did not believe in absolute definition of the term. Prakash Javdekar was also a spokesperson. Ravi Shankar Prasad was the chief of the media department of the BJP. Both became Cabinet ministers. All these BJP spokespersons dutifully obeyed instructions from Gandhinagar to refute allegations leveled against Modi in the run up to the 2014 elections.

Mukhtar Abbas Naqvi was also a BJP spokesperson, but did not become a minister on May 26, 2014. He had committed a couple of mistakes. He had lambasted his own party for seeking to induct Bihar leader Sabir Ali, who had only a few days ago had a long interaction with Modi in Gandhinagar. He also did not obey instructions from Gandhinagar to issue statements against those who made any remarks against Modi. Union Minister Jairam Ramesh in the Manmohan Singh Cabinet had claimed 'Modi talking of sanitation is like Asaram Bapu speaking of chastity' when the then Gujrat chief minister sought to become a mascot of sanitation. Ramesh has his figures on performance of Gujrat on sanitation to make such a claim. Soon BJP spokespersons were asked from Gandhinagar to lampoon Ramesh. Naqvi ignored the instruction. He predictably did not figure in the Modi Cabinet. He was brought back much later when loose cannons within the BJP began spewing venom against Muslims. Modi was brazen enough to pack his Cabinet with 'Yes, Ministers'.

Modi was much more brazen with first Cabinet notification on distribution of portfolios of council of ministers. The notification stated that all policy matters would stay with Prime Minister. This singular act told the Modi model of governance in one single line. All the ministers in his Cabinet were actually Ministers of State and Modi was the only Cabinet Minister for all practical purposes. He unveiled excessive centralization of power in Prime Minister's Office (PMO). The General Budgets and Rail Budgets have all been prepared under the close watch of the PMO. It's normal for secretaries of any ministry being called to the PMO quite frequently and issues pushed without the knowledge of the concerned minister. Indeed, Rajnath Singh is officially Number 2 in the Modi Cabinet. But most of the key decisions and initiatives concerning the Ministry for Home Affairs are being taken in the PMO without the Home secretary kept in the loop.

The ways things have evolved in the Modi government's scheme of things give away an impression that the Prime Minister is wary of or may be paranoid of misdeeds which destroyed the UPA. Hence, ministers are on tight lease and do not enjoy much of discretion as had been the case with A Raja in UPA-II who allegedly scripted the 2G spectrum allocation scam. Yet, Modi cabinet later got a couple of extraordinary talents in Suresh Prabhu (Minister for Railways) and Manohar Parrikar (Minister for Defence). Even while the Ministry of Finance has largely been pedestrian under Jaitely, India's critical sectors of Defence and Railways have begun seeing better days. Even 'Yes, Ministers' Goyal and Javdekar have shown results as well as speed in their respective fields. Modi had completed his journey from chief minister to Prime Minister. He idolized Vajpayee in his public utterances. Yet, he is no Vajpayee and neither does he wanted to become one. His Gujrat model of administration and government paid him rich dividends. For him, there is no reason why he should dump a tested method. When he became chief minister of Gujrat, he had picked his ministers in similar fashion, with the likes of unknown faces Anandiben Patel and Saurabh Patel becoming members of his state council of ministers.

The 2014 mandate also gave fairly large number of saffron robed politicians to 16th Lok Sabha. They largely came from Uttar Pradesh and Rajsthan. Such saffron clad politicians from Uttar Pradesh included fiery Yogi Adityanath, Sakshi Maharaj, Sadhvi Niranjan Jyoti among others. In his first expansion of the council of ministers, Modi picked Sadhvi Niranjan Jyoti due to considerations of her caste and her potential to become a BJP bulwark against Mayawati in Uttar Prdaesh. Adityanath had reason to be crest-fallen, for he had been the most sought after campaigner for the BJP in the state. Sakshi Maharaj was amused with Modi's choice. Hindutva rabble-rousers from the ranks of the BJP in Uttar Pradesh were miffed equally over the choice of the Prime Minister for his Cabinet formation. These loose cannons would soon make people forget that Modi had sought votes on development agenda and on slogan of 'Sabka saath, sabka vikas'.

In the past few decades, tide of foreign funding to Non-Governmental Organisations (NGOs) had been on the rise in quite significant manner. Many of them espoused social and environmental causes. A good number of them were evangelists in the guise of social workers. They worked with tribal in Jharkhand, Chhatisgarh, Odisha and Andhra Pradesh. These states saw missionary schools, nursing homes and hospitals sprouting up and churches too tailed consequently. Rashtriya Swayamsevak Sangh (RSS) woke up much later and sought to compete with them. It propped up Vanwasi Kalyan Ashram to counter the influence of Christian missionaries. It works with tribal for education and health care. But the RSS became well aware that it was no match to the financial muscle of Christian missionaries. More than Muslims, the RSS is concerned about the scale of conversions allegedly carried out by the missionaries in tribal dominated states.

Incidentally, RSS' indoctrination mechanism hinges on twin legs -- Muslim conspiracy to partition India, and attempts to convert Hindus and tribal by missionaries. Saffronites were much alarmed when even Dalits became targets of conversions in Uttar Prdaesh and Bihar. And, thus, miffed BJP leaders unhappy with Modi for making them irrelevant unleashed 'Ghar Wapsi (re-conversion)' campaign in Uttar Pradesh. The campaign had been going on for years without ever attracting attention of the national media. Sulking BJP leaders scaled up the 'Ghar Wapsi' campaign in their bid to embarrass and challenge the might of the new government. Since the agenda had been sponsored by auxiliary wings of the RSS, the Modi government watched the goings on much amused not knowing how to put the genie back in the bottle.

Entire winter session of the Parliament (2014) resonated with musical rhythm of 'Ghar Wapsi'. The Modi government had also ruffled the feathers of Christian politicians in wrong ways in those days. 'He

(Narendra Modi) is a dictator. Can you believe his government sent non-Catholics to represent India when two Indians were canonized by the Pope? Earlier, only Catholics were sent. I called up Sushma Swaraj to tell that never ever non-Catholics had been sent to Pope. But she did not know who had made the decision and expressed helplessness,' Congress leader and former Union minister K V Thomas would lament.

Even while Samajwadi Party chief Mulayam Singh Yadav wondered why was the issue of 'Ghar Wapsi' discussed in the Parliament when there had been no reports to cause worry from his state of Uttar Pradesh. The Parliament spent hours and hours debating the issue. Opposition in the Parliament inadvertently did a world of good to the saffronites by bringing the issue of conversions to the national limelight. Adityanath from the BJP as lead speaker on the issue in Lok Sabha sizzled. A non-apologetic Rajnath Singh threw the idea for a consensus on a national anti-conversion law. He was inspired by erudite Bhartruhari Mahatab of Biju Janata Dal, who told the Lok Sabha that Article 25 of the Constitution, which guarantees freedom to preach and practice faith, was not absolute. 'My freedom ends when my elbow touches someone else,' said Mahatab in Lok Sabha, while recalling spate of conversions of tribal in South Odisha carried out by Missionaries which prompted legislation of an anti-conversion law by the state government, which is now a role model for other states.

Debate was over and so was the 'Ghar Wapsi' campaign. But the government unleashed an unprecedented crackdown against NGOs. Scores of licenses of NGOs were suspended. Others were barred from availing foreign funding. Many of these NGOs were seen by the government being engaged in Missionary activities. The Modi government has not been apologetic about the clampdown against the NGOs. Manmohan Singh in 2012 had given a script for the new government to go against NGOs full throttle. When the environmental activists owing allegiance to various NGOs, including Greenpeace, had virtually laid siege of the Koodankoolam nuclear power plant, Manmohan Singh, the then Prime Minister, had sizzled and launched an unprecedented attack on anti-nuclear power bogey in NGOs. He had accused the NGOs of working at the behest of foreign powers to derail India's bid to grow. Modi took Manmohan Singh's accusations quite seriously, and is pursuing clampdown against the NGOs to the logical end. Greenpeace India is barred from foreign funding, while several others are on the watch list, including the Ford Foundation, which allegedly had links with the NGO of Arvind Kejriwal.

The Modi government is least bothered about the noise made by sympathizers of the NGOs and is determined to weed out the 'black sheep' in due course. This is a favour that he could easily give to the

RSS to buy peace on several other issues, while making anti-industrialization lobby financially starved. Modi showed his brazen ways and also flaunted that he's least bothered of such label.

Rahul Gandhi had thrown his weight behind 'wealthy' farmers of western Uttar Pradesh in 2011. He got a man of his choice in Jairam Ramesh to head Union Ministry for Rural Development. He had his task cut out. He had to get a new law on acquisition of land to replace the then existing one which dated to British times. Ramesh took almost a year to draft Land Acquisition and Rehabilitation and Resettlement Bill. The name did not appeal Gandhi. He wanted stress on fairness in the process of acquisition of land. Consequently, 'The Right to Fair Compensation and Transparency in Land Acquisition, Rehabilitation and Resettlement Bill' was unveiled. The name is such that even ministers have to look at papers to say it properly. But it suggested the whole cause, which Gandhi championed in western Uttar Pradesh. The Parliamentary Standing Committee headed by BJP's Sumitra Mahajan took full one year to give recommendations on the Bill. The Congress would get restless, while Mahajan would test their patience. Yet, the Congress led UPA government never entertained the idea of pushing the bill in the form of an Ordinance. It was only in 2013 and after the government accommodated almost all recommendations of the Opposition parties and the Parliamentary standing committee that the bill was passed by both the Houses of the Parliament.

The bill was conceived with political motives. It proved to be a monster after its birth. Farmers would stall the whole process of land acquisition in anticipation of multi fold of compensation, which the new law promised. Road constructions under public-private-partnership mode were the first casualty. Nitin Gadkari as Union Minister for Road and Surface Transport in the Modi government would launch himself into such a tearing hurries, that a fresh Ordinance would be issued to weed out 'bureaucratic bottlenecks' in the legislation. Not one but the government would bring out three Ordinances on the same subject after two of them lapsed on account of inability of the ruling NDA to get the nod of the Parliament.

The Modi government would not consult any opposition parties on amendments and none would be taken into confidence. Even the NDA allies were briefed at a much later date when the whole world came to know about the government measures. The mindset of the government seemed of -- 'people have given us the mandate, so it's our business to bring what bills we want and in what manner'. In a year, MPs in Indian Parliament would get used to the practice of government springing legislative surprises on them on a regular basis, giving them least time to prepare for discussion or to move amendments. Still, Modi government succeeded in bulldozing legislative lethargy and got quite a good number of bills passed after initial frozen months.

The Opposition suitably gave Modi a well-deserved label of bulldozer.

For first nine months, Union Minister M Venkaih Naidu never missed an opportunity to remind the Congress of its strength of 44 in the Lok Sabha. He would overdo his art of rhyming and would have to apologize in the House once for his acts. His deputy, Minister of State for Parliamentary Affairs, Rajiv Pratap Rudy would be snubbed by Lok Sabha Speaker Sumitra Mahajan for lack of courtesy in the House. The government's relentless bulldozing of the Opposition would get Lok Sabha Speaker in the crossfire as well and her impartiality in the conduct of the House would quite regularly come under the scanner. Modi will show his bulldozer streak with the Opposition in the Parliament, NGOs in the civil society space, and judiciary too by spearheading setting up of the National Judicial Appointments Commission. Incidentally, the Opposition in the Parliament, NGOs in civil society space, and judiciary had forced a lock-down on the Manmohan Singh government on various issues, which even included policy decisions of the government.

Modi has taken significant steps in his first year in the office to ensure elements which forced lock-down on the previous UPA government do not rear their heads in his times. A government in fetters cannot make a nation of billion people take wings to fly in the company of developed nations. Modi knows why Manmohan Singh had failed.

Modi's government could be summed up in 3Bs -- Bold, Brazen, and Bulldozing. With these 3Bs, Modi wants to deter pathological elements within the system, which can rear their heads anytime to hiss and bite and paralyze the system.

Herd Breaker

INDIA is an aggregate of castes and communities.

Kulhariya is a small village by the sides of a state highway in Banka district of Bihar. It borders Jharkhand. Natural wonders in the forms of mountains blasted for decades to source building materials abound in the vicinity. The state highway tells tales of rivers of the area robbed off sands. Laws to curb sand-mining surely seem to have no followers. The place will give an impression as if India was still in the 19th century. Time does not fly at such places, but grinds along with rigors of lives.

The village has large concentration of thatched huts. On the other side of the highway lie paddy fields. As one steps into the paddy field, the little walk through the remains of crops harvested recently becomes a challenge. Wherever one looks for landing of feet, human defecation stares back. The paddy field looks one big open toilet. The sight of Vidya Balan, who was roped in by the government to encourage people not to defecate in the open, flashes in the mind, with freshly splashed and dried up human defecation threatening not to venture further in the field. But journalistic determination hardly succumbs to such repugnant sights. After half an hour of 'trekking', the sight of a dozen elderlies digging out soil emerges. Little closer, they all look much older. They were so old that they should have been spending their times with earnings of their younger times with their grand-children. But the poor of India know no such luxury.

Men in loin clothes were in the company of young women. The sight stood in defiance of the celebrated Indian social traditions. Women were daughters-in law of the men at work and had their saris pulled up to cover their heads in truly traditional Indian ways to guard their honour. The men dug out the soils and the women carried them on their heads to dump at another place. They were digging a micro-irrigation channel. They were paid daily wages under the national level scheme called Mahatma Gandhi National Rural Employment Guarantee Act (MGNREGA). They were Mahadalits, a name given to most economically backward among the scheduled castes of India.

Dalits had been at the bottom of the social strata for ages. For over sixty years since India's Independence, the Congress ruled the country mostly. India's grand old party commanded rock-solid loyalty from the Dalits and Muslims until Rajiv Gandhi frittered away the age old legacy in late 1980s. Sachchar Commission, which was appointed by the government, had claimed in its report that the conditions of the Muslims in India were worse than even the Dalits. The Muslims though were not clubbed with the Mahadalits. Electoral expediency called upon political parties to further segregate the Dalits in their bid to carve out exclusive catchment areas for votes. Mahadalits were such caste groups from within Dalits. The segregated Dalit castes had paid rich electoral dividends to Nitish Kumar in Bihar. In return, a tiny fraction of them got a few square yards of land. They were lucky few. Luck, however, does not bless the mass. Majority of unlucky Mahadalits got a radio set each in lieu of their dedicated voting for Kumar. They were also provided with country liquor shops right outside their habitations so that they could forget their hardships and sleep peacefully after a hard day.

Those dozen Mahadalit labourers of Kulhariya village had been casting their votes for Kumar religiously for past few years. They all gave their ages beyond 60s. The women too shy to speak reluctantly shared their ages and they emerged to be all in their 20s. 'Where are the young men of the village? Why are they not working here in your places,' were questions which touched raw nerves of the elderlies. Drying thick waves of sweats oozing out of their foreheads, they all said in one voice -- 'our sons do not work'. Sugriv Harijan understood that the answer had only confused. 'Our sons got little bit of education. Some of them went to primary schools and some to secondary. They all have no jobs. But they consider themselves educated, and, hence, it would be against their dignity to dig soils here. They loiter around during day times, listening to songs on radio sets given by the government. By dawn, they all get drunk with country liquors. These men and women toil for the youth in their village to get food and liquor,' Harijan made things plain and clear.

His companion Bharat Das nodded in approval. In another neighbouring village, Manoj Kumar was the most sought after Mahadalit youth. He had returned from Delhi where he had worked for a few years as a compounder at a clinic. In his village and also for those in the immediate vicinity, he was a doctor on the call, who prescribed medicines. 'There is no clinic around for a few kilometers and some or others always keep falling ills. I know names of medicines for some common ailments, which come handy for these people,' he would say with pride.

Herd mentality comes natural to the poor and vulnerable sections of the society. The poor hope that their caste leaders for whom they vote would be their protectors. Poverty easily herds people. After the Congress weakened, regional political parties herded castes and communities to perpetuate their brand of politics. Poverty makes people socially vulnerable. Economically well off castes exploit them. Dalits in Uttar Pradesh were such people until Mayawati arrived on the political scene. Dalits do not vote for Mayawati for the sake of development, but for the fact that the dominant caste groups do not dare to bully them for fear of reprisal from the 'iron lady'. The recent two decades of Indian politics saw the vulnerable sections of the society voting for the sake of ensuring their safety from the dominant caste groups.

The Mahadalits of Kulahriya village had heard of Narendra Modi. They shared their thoughts that until their sons got regular jobs their lots would not improve. Modi had become a topic of discussion in their village. They had heard speeches of Modi in makeshift studios, which made rounds of rural areas in Bihar and Uttar Pradesh. It was actually an open air auto-rickshaw with a television set playing out videos of Modi's election speeches.

Bharat Das would say that he was convinced Modi would make jobs for his sons and he would then not have to work in the paddy field to dig out soils day after day.

In Uttar Pradesh, Jatavs have special pride in Mayawati, because she is from their castes. Months before 2014 Lok Sabha elections Jatavs were singing different tunes. 'Sab ko mauka diya...ek mauka to Modi ji ko bhi milna chahiye...Behenji (Mayawati) to PM nahi banengi naa... (all have got opportunities...Modi too should get one...Mayawati can't become PM,' said Dolly, a middle aged Jatav woman near Mathura in Uttar Pradesh, who worked as a sweeper with local municipal corporation but had not been paid salary for three months. She would reason that Mayawati had brought electricity to their homes, but their grown up sons had no jobs.

She too like Bharat Das believed that Modi would make jobs for their sons. Dalits had bolted. They defied stereotypes and began dreaming of better prospects. Modi had emerged as one big hope for them and they too wanted to break free from age old vicious poverty cycle. They could bolt in some ways, because they thought Modi offered them one opportunity to change their economic conditions.

Muslims too had been herded into one political constituency in Uttar Pradesh, Bihar, and West Bengal where they are in such numbers to influence outcome of elections. But they did not bolt. For them the economic progress was secondary and they valued their social security most. The idea to vote for the BJP would be blasphemous for many Muslims. However, there would be a few here and there who would be bold enough to say that they would examine Modi in a fresh manner without the past stereotype affecting their judgments. There would be Muslims in Madhya Pradesh and Gujrat who would openly canvas for the BJP and vote also for the saffron party afterwards. But the Gangetic belt was laboratory of demonization of the BJP to scare the Muslims into a herd constituency.

Uttar Prdaesh was a laboratory where the Muslims saw the BJP as a venomous snake, which could fatally bite them if the party came to power. On Agra-Firozabad highway, Haji Jallo 'Aloowaale', who gave his age 75, would say that he had been voting for Mulayam Singh Yadav of the Samajwadi Party for over two decades. 'Mulayam ko vote karna Allah ki marzi hai (it's Allah's will that we vote for Mulayam),' he said. When he would be told that there had been over 190 communal riots in the last two years under the watch of Yadav in the state, Jallo would say, 'Mulayam ne Masjid to girne nahi dee naa (Mulyam ensured that the mosque was not demolished).' Jallo in his enthusiasm would stop fellow passersby Muslims to ask whom would they vote for in 2014 Lok Sabha elections. Some would say Yadav, which would cheer the old man. Younger lots would say Mayawati, which would make Jallo furious. 'Get out, you scoundrels,' he would scream. Jallo was emotionally bonded to Yadav. But 45 years old Ajgar Hussain Quraisi knew that the Muslims were no more politically united. 'We will vote for Yadav. But young Muslims seem tilting toward Mayawati. The youth believe that Yadav only takes votes and does not give anything in return, he would explain. Modi's name would elicit hatred from the Muslims in Uttar Pradesh. 'Gardan kata sakte haen par Modi ko vote nahi de sakte (We can lose our lives, but can't vote for Modi),' said Muhammed Momeen in Agra. Farther away in Mainpuri district of Uttar Pradesh, the Muslims would have more reasons not to vote for Yadav, because they did not get any benefits. 'We do not get jobs under MGNREGA. We also do not get elderly pension or health care benefits. We will vote for Mayawati,' said 35 years old Dilawar Khan in Konchhi village in Mainpuri.

Muslims in Uttar Pradesh and Bihar had been voting strategically, with single motif to ensure defeat of the BJP candidates. They thought themselves to be politically smart and sought to identify strong anti-BJP candidates in each constituency. They did not know that they had split in big ways by voting for Samajwadi Party, Bahujan Samajwadi Party, and even the Congress. They did not bolt, but were broken.

Traditional voting pattern, as noted by a school teacher and avid political watcher Ram Sewak Yadav in Etah, suggested that en-block Muslim votes could swing fortunes of candidates in as many as 35 Lok Sabha seats in Uttar Pradesh. But he had a caveat, that if non-Muslims and non-Yadavs were to sharply polarise in favour of the BJP then the tactical minority voting would be blunted. 'Narendra Modi PM banega to Gujrat ke tarah yahan bhi tarakki hogi...yahan candidate se hamen matlab nahi...vote Modi ke naam par denge (If Modi becomes PM, even our place will develop like Gujrat. Candidates are not important for us, we will vote for Modi),' Vinod Ghiyar in his 30s said in Mainpuri district in Uttar Pradesh. Ram Sewak Yadav's caveat looked playing out as innumerable other backward and extremely backward castes rallied behind Modi in the 2014 elections. Modi became Prime Minister because he could win votes of those who had never voted for the BJP. He appealed to those who had been herded for ages, first by the Congress and then by regional caste centric parties.

Socio-economic conditions of the poor make them to expect miracles form the political class in quick time. They are not the people blessed with the gift of patience. They have a bouquet of choices to make when it comes to cast their votes. Their lives are spent in search for means to meet their basic needs. They are millions of poor in India who hope that one day their ballots would change their fortunes. It's nothing short of a miracle that their hopes never die despite six decades of deceit. Their faith in the Indian democracy has only increased over the years. Elites in urban centres who check weather conditions before thinking of venturing out of comforts of their homes to cast votes stereotyped millions of poor as ones who sold their ballots for liquor and money. Elites of India have monstrous disconnect with realities. India's irony is that the voice of the elites is heard the most. They are easily available everywhere. One needs to make quite an effort to listen to the voice of the poor. Unless they trust their audience, they do not tell their tales.

The corporate world thought that Modi would give Indian economy a rocket ride soon after assuming charge. In place, they found to their dismay that Modi was a man of incremental changes. He was in no hurry to slog the economy to higher trajectory. No 'big bang' was unveiled in the first two Budgets of the new government. There was no fundamental change to the economy either. 'People had not given mandate for incrementalism, but for fundamental changes. What Modi is doing could have been done by any government even if they did not command a majority in the Lok Sabha,' said a secretary in the Government of India (GoI). Big bang in the Indian economy had happened during the times of PV Narsimha Rao. Atal Bihari Vajpayee's inauguration in the office was itself on the big bang note. He began with 'smile of the Buddha' in Pokhran (1998). Sooner the world clamped sanctions on India. When you are at a crossroad, you choose a new direction. Vajpayee brought in fundamental change to the India economy, but in continuity to what Rao had done.

But Modi faced no such crisis to unveil the big bang ideas for the economy. He found that Manmohan Singh had left too many ideas for structural changes for him to pursue. The change in government did not disrupt economic continuity. Modi had to demonstrate that he could take decisions. He began taking decisions in truck-loads. Heavy blanket of policy paralysis lying over the Indian economy was lifted. Two decades of economic reforms had pitfalls too. Poverty held its grounds in the last one decade. Distress of economically vulnerable sections only compounded. Youth in rural areas were armed with school and college certificates, but had no jobs. They had no skills either to think beyond the government jobs. Doors of banks were shut on them. They did not benefit from the economic reforms of previous two decades.

Dalits, Mahadalits and Muslims failed to stake their claims on the pie of the gains India saw from two decades of economic reforms. India saw alarming widening of gap between 'haves' and 'have nots'. Economic prosperity made out of economic reforms reached only the state capitals. Large parts of the state in various parts of the country were dark zones which were yet to be dotted by economic prosperity. Modi had appealed those souls in the dark zones during the election campaign for the 2014 battle. Modi first needs to deliver on promises made to millions of people to bring changes in their lives. He needs to execute answers to his own questions, which he asked during election trails: 'Why should people dig soils even after six decades of Indian Independence.' The answer to the question is not in the immediate vicinity. But if ambitious plan of imparting skills to 500 million youth by 2022 could see light of the day, substantive changes may occur on ground.

Even Manmohan Singh government wanted to skill India, but the plan was on paper only. Even after one year of Modi in the office, arguably nothing has been done to suggest India has embarked on the path of a skilled nation. Merely talking about it would be of not much help, as time flies, leaving trails of inaction as footprints in memories of the people. In the last two decades, China came all over India to destroy traditional crafts. Cheap sells and China sold everything from sewing needles to toys, from decorative lights to idols, from kitchen appliances to home decorations, and many more. Indian artisans have shut their shops. They have lost their patrons, who have shifted to the cheap Chinese dumped products. The two ways trade between India and China is now close to $100 billion, which includes roughly $48 billion of trade deficit for India. China is in a position to dump its goods in India, because it has a strong skilled manpower that can produce things at such levels to stay profitable by indulging in volume business. India will arguably take decades to match capacity and scale of China.

Modi's twin planks of 'Make in India' and 'Skilled India by 2022' are ambitious and game changing ideas. They are, however, not his unique contributions. They were flagship campaign of the Manmohan Singh government. Difference is in commitment and Modi government has shown intention to take them forward in serious manners. The scale of seriousness could be gauged from the fact, that China has unveiled 'Make in China 2025' campaign under which it would seek transformation of its manufacturing abilities. China is global manufacturing hub already and still the nation wants transition to next higher level. India has woken up at least three decades late to seek to ride the manufacturing bus. India will have to act fast and will need to expedite 'Skilled India' campaign with much more seriousness. Modi's twin planks make for a good script for electoral politics as well, because he was able to break the herd of caste electorates only after he ignited dreams of prosperity in classes, which had been at the bottom of the economic pyramid for ages.

People gave a mandate to Modi for five years. The mandate will be up for renewal in 2019. His visions to turnaround directions of the country, however, overstep tenure of people's mandate. Swachh Bharat (Clean India) has a deadline of 2019. Housing for all has a deadline of 2022. The timeline to clean 2500 km long river Ganga is 18 years. Skilled India has a deadline of 2022. Make in India campaign will arguably take quite a while for people on the grounds to relate to its tangible gains. His government wants to cut the population dependent on agriculture by half, though with no timeline. This will obviously be linked to collateral benefits from 'Make in India' and 'Skilled India' initiatives. The agrarian stress is largely because the land is not irrigated and cost of farming is too high while being dependent on vagaries of Monsoon.

Within weeks of his inauguration, Modi unveiled an ambitious scheme 'Pradhan Mantri Grameen Sinchai Yojna', which seeks to reach waters to farmers for irrigation. Even after one year of the Modi government, bureaucracy is still working out nitty gritty of the scheme. It took 15 months for the Modi Cabinet to finally clear the scheme. His first year in office has seen farmers' distress because of poor Monsoon firstly and spates of unseasonal rains and hailstorms afterwards. Farmers' distress has already been lapped by the Opposition to mobilize their demoralized cadres. The speed of decision making by Modi is yet to be matched by the bureaucracy. Disconnect between intention and action is too palpable.

The full first year in the office saw schemes and plans of the decade long Manmohan Singh reign dusted off and re-packaged. The Nandan Nilekani spearheaded unique identity enumeration through 'Aadhar' became buzz word for the Modi government. The financial inclusion, which had been dormant in Manmohan Singh's times, suddenly found a marketing wizard in Modi. In a span of a few months, 100 million bank accounts were opened for those who were out of the banking footprints under Jan Dhan scheme. Direct Benefit Transfer (DBT) of various subsidy programme was envisaged by the Manmohan Singh government. But the Modi government would make DBT a talking point. Near the end of the first year in the office, his government would unveil a bouquet of social security schemes through bank accounts opened under Jan Dhan scheme. 'Aadhar' would be the carrier of all such programme. The LPG subsidy is being passed on to beneficiaries through 'Aadhar' seeded bank accounts. Modi launched 'Give it Up' campaign' for the affluent classes to self-exclude themselves from the LPG subsidy coverage. He has set a target of 10 million people giving up the subsidy. There are about 150 million LPG consumers in India. No one talked of giving up the LPG subsidy until Modi arrived on the scene. Indian billionaires came forward and publicly stated that they had given up the LPG subsidy and asked their employees to do so. Irony is that none seriously thought to ask the affluent to self-exclude from various subsidy schemes before Modi. Two million LPG consumers gave up the subsidy and the number is still counting. Transfer of LPG subsidy through DBT has netted $1.25 billion in savings. Modi told industrial houses and bankers, that if 10 million people were to give up the LPG subsidy an equal number of poor would get access to clean energy. Decades of subsidy regime did not make meaningful interventions in the lives of the poor, because three-fourth of it was pocketed by unscrupulous elements and those who did not deserve it. The middle class could get angry with such measures, but only a bold leadership can correct structural and ideological distortions in the subsidy policy of India.

The thought to bring rationality in pricing of services is spreading in other wings of the government. Mumbai sub-urban Railways carry six and a half million commuters a day. They pay token price for availing services of the Railways. Majority of them are office-goers in Mumbai, which is the financial capital of the country. The commuters demand better services, including air-conditioned trains. But the Railways would not be able to charge them fairly, because local political groups can bring the metropolitan city to a halt. Same is the case with Kolkata. But office-goers all claim transport allowances, which should be adequate enough to compensate for the cost of commuting. Even if 50 per cent of six and a half million daily commuters get transport allowances, then Railways because of fear of local political parties has actually been subsidizing employers. Is that fair, asked an official in the Ministry of Railways, suggesting why not segregate daily wage and livelihood earners, who are actually poor, from those who are well off and who can recover higher cost of transportation from their employers. If this could be done, Railways would have additional resources to invest and improve services for the passengers. Modi has shown intent to bite the bullet and in coming times non-deserving classes would be excluded from many of the indirect subsidy programmes.

The only way to broad-base economic growth in the country is through the government significantly jacking up public investment. This is being done through kick-starting infrastructure development not only in road and rail, but many other areas, including logistic and warehousing development, agriculture and rural infrastructure. But major impetus to the growth story which can give political dividends on a sustainable basis will come only if the unemployed youth in the semi-urban and rural areas take up businesses and engage in gainful employments to produce and add values to goods, which can access markets nearby and elsewhere.

The Modi government's second Budget unveiled Mudra banking to lend financial instruments to those who have not yet been served by banking institutions. With a corpus of roughly $16 billion, Mudra bank could give a major fillip to millions of youth wasting their lives in search of opportunities. Supplemented by technology and skill incubation centres, which should come up at major places within each state, Mudra bank should emerge as an engine to birth entrepreneurs across length and breadth of the country. Decades ago the government did a lot of activities to incubate entrepreneurs in Kakinada in Andhra Pradesh, time has surely come for many such experiments. China could become factory of the world, because the government there owned stakes in initiatives of entrepreneurs. If an entrepreneur incubation centre gives a go ahead for setting up of an enterprise, the government institutions should own at least 20 per cent shares and shoulder responsibility to absorb at least one fifth of products manufactured by them through assured market linkage programmes. China has done this and it is surely doable in India as well.

The likes of Anand Mahindra could be asked to do a Nandan Nilekani for birthing millions of entrepreneurs in semi-urban and rural areas.

Nilekani's 'Aadhar' enumeration is helping Modi save billions of dollars. The bureaucracy had opposed tooth and nail his endevours, but could roll out a gigantic exercise only because of unconditional support of Manmohan Singh. Modi could initiate another such venture by picking up someone from the industry who has zeal to do an indelible job for the country. He will find a platform in millions of semi-trained personnel of India's Self-Help Group (SHG) as well as young traders in various locations ready to ride such a bandwagon. The Mudra bank and the initiative of 'Skilled India 2022' could become handy in spearheading birthing of India's millions of entrepreneurs. Why not begin with a body on the lines of Unique Identification Authority of India (UIAI), which gave 'Aadhar'? The financial savings made out of rationalization of direct and indirect subsidy programmes should be pumped into the exercise to make millions of youth employers. While Make in India campaign would largely attract big foreign manufacturing, small scale industries should become rallying cry of new generation of entrepreneurs guided by the government.

Modi broke caste herds in 2014 elections, because he came up with an economic vision. The Muslims who have been one rock-solid herd electorates are watching him from sidelines. They have enough reasons and many well justified to be cynical about the BJP. Modi had vowed that he would not let any to touch the honour of the Muslims. His famous statement was '...kisi ko bhi kisi ki pagdi nahi uchhalne denge (...will not allow any to play with honour of anybody)'. He has to crack his whip on too many loose mouths within the ranks of his party.

If he could unleash the next wave of the economic expansion, which genuinely witnesses participation of people from the ranks of Dalits, Mahadalits, Extremely Backward Castes, and Muslims, Modi would become the first politician in India to have risen above the caste and community considerations. He broke the herds. He has to ensure they do not again become herds.

Bouddhik men

INDIA's history and culture lived through oral tradition for ages, and that explains natural talent of its people for oratory.

Until Atal Bihari Vajpayee became Prime Minister, India knew of an orator among the political class. After becoming Prime Minister, silence bug strikes occupants of the 7, Race Course Road in New Delhi. For almost one and a half decades, India at large did not hear the political class connecting with the masses. Oratory succumbed to shrillness. Public space looked quarrelsome and full of cacophony. Hardly any spoke the voice of the people and sought to connect with them. New Delhi seemed utterly disconnected with India.

After losing the 2009 opportunity to step into the shoes of his friend Vajpayee, the political horizon of LK Advani lost most of its space. He looked a political leader whose audience was drawn from the comforts of the Lutyen's Delhi. Like others, who become slave to New Delhi, he too became a Shah Alam-II in whose time the Mughal sultanate shrunk to an area between Red Fort in Old Delhi to Palam, which now hosts the airport. In Advani's political sultanate none existed beyond New Delhi. Advani was not alone and he symbolized the larger disease with which the political class was stricken. The Congress suffered from this disease more acutely. The comforts of the political class in New Delhi had dulled them to such an extent that they ceased to connect with the people. They spoke only at election times, and they narrated the same old story whose script had lost the sense of time.

After a few years, Narendra Modi began laying siege to New Delhi from Ahmedabad. Later, Advani certified that Modi is a great event manager. Modi need not be pleased, for he knew it was hardly a compliment. Advani was not alone in viewing Modi as an event manager. The media, which is the custodian of the public opinion, also suffered from the same bug, which struck the political class. The world of the Indian media was (is) not much better than the geographical expanse of Shah Alam-II. Indian journalism in the last one and a half decades bore strong imprints of the 'celebrity' news anchors and their siblings in the newspapers. They flaunted their reach to the top brass of the political class, bureaucracy, and business. The media largely savoured Advani's left-handed compliment to Modi of a great even manager. The media too thought the Modi campaign to lay siege to New Delhi as an advertisement blitzkrieg. That Modi used the latest technological tools to connect with the people on a largescale came handy for the New Delhi media and the political class of the same tribe to parrot the Advani line. Predictably, Modi after becoming Prime Minister treated both the political class and the media stricken with the New Delhi bug with disdain.

India appears awe-struck to Modi's oratory. The larger Indian Diaspora is in knots. The world has heard of Modi. He has sought to question the status quo in the world order, besides asking developed world to respond to Indian concerns. He charms with depth of his oratory and yet confronts the audience with straightforward approach. Chinese President Xi Jinping has seen Modi as charmer and brutally straightforward as well. Pakistani premier Nawaz Sharif has been left in Catch 22 situations whether to embrace Modi on a path of collective development of South Asia and forget the issue of Kashmir or let Raheel Sharif fire those shots at the international border to keep the bilateral relations 'warm'.

Modi owes his oratory and candour to his Rashtriya Swayamsewak Sangh (RSS) pedigree. It's not that he is first from the RSS pedigree to connect with the people. It's also not that Modi is the only oratory from the stable of the BJP. Sushma Swaraj, Arun Jaitely, Rajnath Singh, and Uma Bharti are among the notable orators of the saffron party. There is no better combative orator around then Swaraj. There is no better destroyer with the acumen of a lawyer then Jaitely. Singh sometimes may remind of Vajpayee. And Bharti was a firebrand oratory, though rusted by the upheavals of her tumultuous political career. Yet, they did not rise enough to connect with the people with new script. They were in league with Advani. Their political canvas was not big enough.

Bouddhik (intellectual talks) is most coveted of responsibilities in the scheme of things of the RSS. It's not that all get to give Boudhik during morning Shakha (open classes) of the RSS. Sometimes lazybones among the RSS functionaries would be asked to give Boudhik as token punishment. But largely it will be the forte of the best mind in the RSS stable. Vajpayee was one such regular for Bouddhik. Old timers in the RSS recall Vajpayee as a naughty activist who would indulge in pranks too often. Besides, his eyes would mostly be set on food. Knowing well his nature, Vajpayee's mentors in those days assigned him the onus to give Bouddhik. Later, he earned the fame of the best Bouddhik giver. This 'punishment' helped him hone his oratory. He could speak for hours. He would regale his audiences with the depth of his knowledge, served with humour. The poet in him made his oratory laced with satires. Subsequently, Vajpayee became 'Hriday Samrat (king of heart)'. He was one of those rare orators after Pandit Jawaharlal Nehru.

The RSS morning Shakhas are incomplete without a Bouddhik session. The RSS functionaries pride in listening to counter viewpoints. They'll debate and discuss. Yet, they will hold their grounds. They will listen to the counterpoints to further sharpen their arguments against them. The RSS gives equal importance to mental sharpness, besides stressing on physical fitness. Even those who have done pratham varsh (one year) would be much at ease giving talks and engaging others in discussions. And those who have done tritiya varsh (three years) would invariably be intellectually sharp enough to speak on issues for hours. They would not need notes to make their speeches. They grow up to become natural speakers. Even if an RSS functionary has not got formal education but has attended these morning Shakhas for a few years would come out well informed about the issues. The RSS Shakhas are open laboratory of mental and physical skills, which dot the lanes and bylanes of India.

After the Hindutva took backseat in socio-political space, the RSS too began losing sheen. The full impact of India embracing liberalization in 1990s was felt in a few years' times. Urbanization picked up the momentum. The young men and women flocked to the large urban centres. The jobs were not elsewhere. Homes in small towns and villages resembled empty nests. The educated lots had no time for activities not connected with their pursuits to get better employments. The RSS too felt the impact. The Shakhas looked deserted. The Bouddhik audiences got thinner each passing days. The Shakhas in small towns stared into the prospects of becoming those empty nests which had hit the society with the full force. The RSS admitted the challenge and sought to find ways to connect with the young men. It found the social networking options useful. Its offices even in small towns boasted of computers in late 1990s. Subsequently, the mobile phone revolution made its task to connect with the people a lot easier. It found much to the relief that the changing times offered opportunities and the RSS lapped them by both the hands.

The rapid urbanization also left trains of lifestyle ailments. The obesity in the children acquired pandemic proportions. In large urban centres, lifestyle diseases affected people in alarming number. Even before Baba Ramdev made people to rub their nails at public places in hopes of reversing graying hairs to their original splendor and getting community parks full of those who rhythmically contracted and expanded their bellies in efforts to lose weight, the RSS Shakhas drilled volunteers to embrace martial Yogic Aasans (postures) for physical fitness. Soon, people began flocking to the RSS Shakhas in good numbers at urban centres. Parents of obese children began sending their wards to the RSS Shakhas. Those who were worried about their kids' lack of discipline found the RSS Shakhas as options to inculcate better behavior in them.

The RSS' penchant for discipline is legendary. Those who break its unwritten laws become history for the organization in quick time. KN Govindacharya's mistake was just that he spoke what was a fact, but he fell from the most powerful position in the BJP to anonymity in a matter of days. When Vajpayee was Prime Minister, Govindacharya had one of those rare slip of guard and had called him a 'mukhauta (mask)'. Even Advani could not escape the wrath of the RSS when he discovered Muhammed Ali Jinnah to be a secular leader when he was at his mausoleum during his Pakistan visit. He had to quit from the post of the BJP president in quick time.

The wheels of the RSS keep rolling because of an army of volunteers who renounce their respective family and swear to stay bachelor all life. They dedicate their life for the cause of the society and the nation. They live selfless lives. They do not seek monetary gains. They are called 'pracharaks (preachers)'. India has two of them as Prime Ministers so far, which include Vajpayee and Modi. The Haryana chief minister Manohar Lal Khattar also hails from this army of bachelor. The RSS is unforgiving if any pracharak midway discovers yearning for emotional comforts in opposite sex and seeks family life. Advani was an exception, who, though a pracharak, was persuaded to get married at quite an advanced age just to ensure that his family tree survived. He was the only surviving member in his family who had migrated to India from Sindh in Pakistan.

One pracharak in a large city fell in love and sought permission for marriage. Permission never came his way and he was banished from the RSS. The consequence was such that all those who knew him deserted in quick time. He faced a kind of social boycott. The matter came to such a level that he had to leave the city to begin his life afresh. The RSS has an answer to why it's unforgiving to such yearnings for course-correction by a pracharak. 'They are accepted in homes and invited for meals and sometimes even offered stay by the people because of their status as bachelor. If they were to take advantage of such positions for goals not meant for them, they surely harm trusts, which if broken cannot be repaired,' said one RSS functionary.

The RSS had enough goodwill to establish connect with the people after losing much of the sheen in the late 1990s. Long Congress rule acts as tonic for the RSS to add fat. The nests did not look empty. The RSS knew ways to stay relevant in the changing times. It only became stronger. It stayed relevant by connecting with the people on issues affecting their lives.

The RSS does not believe that politics alone can bring change in the country and the society. In fact, the RSS is of the belief that politics is one of many ways to achieve the goals it sets for its functionaries. In its social outreach, the RSS works with tribal by running schools and clinics for them. It runs vocational courses in cities. It offers educational aides. It has hostels in big cities. There is no area in which the RSS has no presence. It engages with the intellectuals. Academicians take part in discussions on issues at the RSS functions, which would mostly be close-door. Doctors in the city would work with the RSS. Lawyers would engage with the RSS. The college students would be the energetic flag-bearers of the ideology of the RSS. It would have wings for women as well. The RSS would look to most as one large moral and cultural guardian.

Unlike others the RSS would walk miles to connect with ideological adversaries. In the scheme of the things, the RSS would make bridges even with those who would otherwise see it as an enemy. And, thus, there will be no surprise that leaders like Sharad Yadav, Mulayam Singh Yadav, Lalu Prasad, and Sharad Pawar would have many friends from the ranks of the RSS. Even while the RSS will have the vision of a 'Hindu Rashtra' as its core vision and 'Garv se kaho hum Hindu haen (say with pride we're Hindus)' as principal slogan, the saffron outfit has made bridges with Muslims and their organizations.

The RSS has such an overwhelming network that it becomes a powerful mode of swinging opinions in the times of elections. The RSS is not just soul but even body of the BJP. Sometimes it stays aloof elections as part of tactical retreat. But it gets electrified on a few occasions to manage back-stage elections of the BJP candidates. The Lok Jan Shakti Party (LJP) chief Ram Vilas Paswan, who had walked out of the Vajpayee

Cabinet in 2002 on the issue of the post-Godhra riots, had to reach out to the RSS functionaries to bail out the party candidates in the 2014 Lok Sabha elections who were not getting the ground support due to their image of being musclemen.

One RSS pracharak, who was in-charge of a zone in Bihar, called a Lok Sabha candidate of the Mayawati led BSP from the Sasaram constituency known to the world as place from where the Congress leader and daughter of Jagjivan Ram, Meira Kumar contested. On phone the BSP candidate spoke in manners to suggest that he had the utmost respect for the RSS functionary. His ticket was withdrawn due to reasons well known in the BSP. He asked the RSS functionary what could he do for him and when told that since he was no more contesting the elections would he work for the BJP nominees in the region. 'Now that you've told me, I am at your service with all my resources,' he told the RSS functionaries. He was with strong following on the ground and he lent his weight to BJP's nominee Chedi Paswan, who trounced Meira Kumar from the Sasaram constituency.

The RSS had invested all its energy and resources for Modi. The RSS' zeal for Modi was not matched by its efforts for Advani in 2009 or the re-election bid of Vajpayee in 2004. On both the occasions the RSS was less impressed in manners in which the two iconic leaders had transformed themselves after coming in power. They had not lived up to the expectations of the RSS.

The RSS took great pride in Vajpayee. He was the first from the ranks who reached the Lok Sabha. Vajpayee helped the RSS to shed the taint of an organization of (Nathuram) Godse (who killed Mahatma Gandhi). Vajpayee brought the RSS into the social mainstream. His political acumen and flexibility to adapt to the immediate challenges made even socialists to work hand-in-hand with the RSS functionaries. Many socialists won elections in 1977 because of the hard work of the RSS functionaries on the grounds. Vajpayee was the RSS' golden boy. He was loved, adored and admired. His follies were looked away. He was an asset worthy to be weighed in gold for the RSS. But Vajpayee faltered in achieving the goals of the RSS. Indian political system consumed Vajpayee. For the RSS, Vajpayee looked not any different than a Congress leader.

In Modi, the RSS sees its best man at the front. The RSS chief Mohan Bhagwat has said that Modi is that Abhimanyu who would demolish the chakravyuh (trapping). Vajpayee was obviously also an Abhimanyu, but he could not clear the chakravyuh. Not only in personal life (Vajpayee lived a family life, with an adopted daughter around), Modi is much different than Vajpayee. For Modi, the RSS is not just a moral guardian, but life in itself. He as an adolescent embraced the RSS. His worldview is shaped by the RSS. He lived the RSS for most parts of his life. Unlike Vajpayee, who looked more of a politician, Modi has stayed an RSS man despite his long stints as chief minister of Gujrat and now Prime Minister of India. Even while India looks awe-struck with ideas of Modi, those who have seen the RSS closely know that they all have been spoken in the morning Bouddhik for years. The RSS' socio-economic philosophy has found in Modi its most potent propagator.

The economic prescription of the RSS functionaries would sound no different than what the Left parties espouse for, but for one exception. The Left parties espouse the state to own the enterprises. The RSS would differ here with the Left and argue that the government has to facilitate the business and enterprises to grow and would lay stress on 'improving ease of doing business'. Ever since Modi has become Prime Minister, he has been talking only of improving the ease of doing business.

The New Delhi bug stricken media would believe that Modi has outgrown the RSS. That he's a super autocrat who has abrogated the idea of collective leadership. The RSS is least concerned about day to day functioning of the government. It wants the idea of economic self-sufficiency pursued by the government. The Modi government has accordingly unveiled the campaign for 'Make in India', besides 'Skilled India' to cut down the dumping of the Chinese goods. The RSS would want India to engage Pakistan, but without the issue of Kashmir coming on the table. The RSS would want the issue of Pakistan illegally annexed parts of Kashmir to come into discussion. The Modi government has exactly done that, besides telling China in most unequivocal manner that its business in Pakistan Occupied Kashmir is unfriendly. The RSS wants India to reform agriculture and make a transition to organic farming, besides checking excessive use of fertilizers in vogue due to urea subsidy. The Modi government is dot on the line. The RSS wants the education to be 'Indianized' on the grounds that Macaulay turned India into a British colony in perpetuity. Modi planted Smriti Irani as Union Minister for Human Resources Development and she is more zealous than any RSS functionary is pursuing the agenda. The RSS argued for many years that India should be self-sufficient in defence production. Modi again is dot on the line in giving a push to such a goal. And, hence, it's quite ignorant of those who say that the RSS is micro-managing the affairs of the Modi government, for there is no need at all.

In the intervening period when the 2014 verdict came and inauguration of Modi as Prime Minister, the RSS headquarter in Jhandewalan buzzed with a lot of activities. The wannabe BJP leaders descended there in good numbers. Some even dashed to Nagpur. In the end the council of ministers headed by Modi consisted of those who had deep roots in the RSS, besides a few who were skillfully defending the BJP mascot in the run up to the elections. Likes of Rajnath Singh, Nitin Gadkari, Dharmendra Pradhan, Radha Mohan Singh, Kalraj Mishra, Giriraj Singh among others wear their RSS pedigree on their sleeves.

After the RSS held a conclave of its affiliate organizations in the Vasant Kunj area of New Delhi for three days in which ministers after ministers made a beeline to impress upon the delegates of the work being done, a section of the media, besides other political parties, about the scale of the involvement of the saffron mentor in the affairs of the government. Their outcry bared their sense of disconnect with reality beyond New Delhi. Modi himself went to the conclave on the last day and won a pat from the saffron mentor for the way he was running the affairs of the government.

The RSS is so overwhelming for the BJP that many rags to riches story ring in the ears of those who have seen the saffron outfit from close quarters. Senior among of the RSS pracharaks attract a few of the youth who associate themselves with them as their assistants. They are assigned works like helping the pracharak in running his appointments or taking care of their meals by cooking or travelling with them as companions. In late 1990s one youth struggling for his livelihoods attached with a senior RSS functionary who had risen to a powerful position in the BJP. The youth was essentially a loafer in his home town and his family wanted him to be away for fear to his life. In a few years after staying with the powerful RSS functionary turned BJP leader, the youth began amassing wealth. Subsequently, he had enough wealth and acquaintances within the BJP that he staked claims for a Lok Sabha ticket. He got the ticket and won the elections as well. He is now three time Lok Sabha MPs and owns palatial Kothis in New Delhi's posh localities, besides investments overseas.

The BJP is full of leaders who were seen riding scooters not many years ago, but now own choppers and palatial houses. Some of them when they begin campaigning at the time of elections bring truck-load of mineral waters in their constituencies, besides booking hundreds of SUVs, which they give to each of the key local party workers to canvass. During the time the BJP was in power with Vajpayee as the head of the government, quite a few of the party leaders made riches in quick time. The NDA government (1998-04) was pump priming the economy with billions of dollars poured in the infrastructure sector, besides dismantling the Inspector Raj in the economy. Such BJP leaders acted as middle men to broker deals for the corporate houses and in lieu of their services made quick bucks. Therefore, the RSS believed that Vajpayee was not much different from the Congress leaders. He could not take on the rot which had set into the system.

Modi too was attached to senior RSS functionaries when he was still a young boy. He swept floors of their rooms and cooked for them. His life stayed modest even when he had become an important BJP functionary. He had seen from close quarters those within the BJP acting like their siblings in the Congress to make wealth when the party came to power. He had spent enough time in New Delhi to know the ways of the fixers wearing the clothes of the politicians. He suited the most in the scheme of the things of the RSS to break the shackles of the New Delhi Caucus over the government and politics.

Modi must have been passionate about Bouddhik during his days in the RSS. He has carried his passion to his 7, Race Course Road office. He charmed Indian Diaspora at Maddison Square in the US. He extended his Bouddhik charm to Sydney. He floored Canadians and Indian Diaspora in Vancouver. He had his cricket stadium filled audience in Dubai lapping each of his words. His address to students of the Fudan University in China was much talked about. At home, Modi has revived people's connection with radio. His 'Mann ki Baat" in which even the US President Barack Obama featured once has been a regular feature. He was bold enough to break off from the fixed format of the Prime Minister's address on Independence Day from the ramparts of the Red Fort to set agenda for the nation and utilize the annual opportunity to push powerful social messages. In his first address he set the target to ensure toilets in each government school across the country and by the next address he reported that the target had been met. In Haryana, he would call upon the people with folded hands to not kill the girl child in the fetus. His call for 'SelfieWithDaughter" ran as wildfire not just in India but worldwide and people in various countries proudly posed with their daughters and shared their selfies.

Incidentally, Modi sticks to the Bouddhik mode of communication in which he is assured of audience. His Bouddhik spark as a communicator was seen on a few occasions in the Parliament. But after the Congress struck to the strategy to troop into the well of the House the moment the party members saw him coming, Modi began shunning the Parliament. With the shrill in the Parliament growing with each passing days, Modi would skip the Lok Sabha and Rajya Sabha. He surely looked a communicator to a committed audience. With the Monsoon session of the Parliament in his second year in the office nearly washed out due to the Opposition baying for blood of Sushma Swaraj, Shivraj Singh Chouhan, and Vasundhara Raje on issues of Lalitgate and Vyapam scam, Modi gave the Parliament a total miss. Even while Swaraj sizzled with her combativeness in tearing apart the Congress with counter charges against the acts of omission and commission of the Gandhi family while defending charges against her in the Lok Sabha amidst pandemonium, Modi did not think proper to be present in the House to lend the moral weight behind his senior Cabinet colleague.

True to the RSS tradition, Modi is much at ease making friends among his political rivals. He effortlessly made friendship with Lalu Prasad and Mulayam Singh Yadav. Modi literally grabbed Nitish Kumar's hands on the occasion of the wedding of the daughter of Prasad and since then they are back on talking terms. Mamata Banerjee, who for a year after Modi becoming Prime Minister made it sure that she neither met him nor sent any of her minister to meetings called by the Centre or the NITI Aayog. 'When will the chief minister of West Bengal meet the Prime Minister of the country,' was a poser to her to which she ducked saying: 'The question does not pertain to the issue being discussed right now.' However, Modi won her over soon and afterwards she not only called on Modi, but even accompanied him to his historic visit to Bangladesh. She allowed Modi to script history by getting the Indo-Bangladesh Land Boundary Agreement ratified. In the run up to the 2014 Lok Sabha elections, she called Modi a 'Dangai (rioter)'. A year after Modi's inauguration, Trinamool Congress is close to becoming part of extended NDA. Modi surely demonstrated ease to win friends and co-opt his political rivals into working relationship.

Yet, Modi has no space for the Congress in his bid to co-opt the political rivals. The RSS too has a penchant to stay away from the Congress leaders. The Congress historically had sought to destroy the RSS. The enmity is mutual. And, Modi carries the legacy in full force.

The RSS was particular when charting out the leadership transition when the 2014 elections was still long distance to get an outsider to head the BJP. Nitin Gadkari was brought in to head the BJP at such time. Till then, Gadkari was not a name with which people in New Delhi were familiar with. Later, he was introduced as the man who built roads and bridges in Maharashtra as the state minister. He was a bulky man, with fat bulging out from each part of his body, when he assumed charge of the BJP chief at the Ashoka Road office. He was comfortable talking business. He would arrange journalists from New Delhi to come to Nagpur and see his business acumen in running sugar mills, with farmers enlisted in co-operatives. His vision would be that each politician should be like a businessman and create jobs for others. Soon, his business interests consumed him, and he had to leave the post of the BJP chief. His exit from the top BJP post was a setback for the RSS, for its bid to free the party from the New Delhi caucus yielded no results.

The RSS' last hope in curing the BJP from the New Delhi bug was in Modi. The saffron mentor believed in Modi's brazen streak to take head on the New Delhi bug. In the game of bullfight, you've to be bull-headed to stand any chance for win.

And, the bull-headed does not have too many friends, and often has enough enemies.

DREAM-WALKING

THE war sometimes is won much before actual battle is even fought.

The 2014 electoral battle was fought among the unequal. There was one warrior against whom opponents fought to ensure he did not emerge the general of his outfit. Once he was anointed the general, his opponents laid their arms even before the battle was fought. The general crushed a fragmented and defeated army of opponents with an envious ease. The 2014 electoral battle may be recorded as massacre of political opponents in a scale not seen for decades.

The 2019 re-run of the battle would have a new script. The battle would be fought on new terms. Tables would have turned. The victorious general of the 2014 would have to climb a mountain before he faces his opponents. He himself built a mountain of expectations higher than the Himalayas. His each step to climb up the mountain would be examined and reviewed with magnified lenses. His follies would be lampooned. His excesses would be lapped with much glee. His opponents would plan and scheme to tear apart the facade that he would seek to build. His opponents would re-group. They know that 69 per cent of the votes, which did not go to the victorious general of the 2014 battle, could be united. He will have to see that his 31 per cent vote share, which was lowest for any political formation to reach the magical figure of past 272 of a comfortable majority, increases not marginally but significantly. His opponents may not always stay fragmented, for they know that they would be decimated if they remain divided. They have lessons in plenty to learn by the time the plot for the 2019 battle gets ready.

Modi was the ferocious general of the 2014 battle. In his next battle, he would have to check how many of his weapons rusted and blunted. He may fatigue. He may tire. Fatigue may strike his audience. People may get tired of his repetitiveness. His opponents may replenish. His opponents may wither away also. Modi scripted a fairy tale on a clean slate. He had an advantage, because his predecessor had left a tarred legacy. Dreams which ballooned in the minds of millions of people would seek their reflections on the slate by the time he goes into another battle. He will no more have the luxury to go with a clean slate. He will have to show that the glass is at least half filled and another journey he would need to embark on to make it full. Time will not test him only, but his opponents as well. There are too many of his opponents around. Some of them will wither away in the natural course. But many of them will stay to fight another battle.

Rahul Gandhi will arguably be his principal opponent. He is seeking to re-invent himself. He has come back after his 57 days long sabbatical from an undisclosed destination with full vigour. His public perception is in abyss. His leadership has been a fiasco. There are too many rumblings within the Congress against his impending elevation to the post of the party president. Gandhi's elevation will mark an end to an era of Sonia Gandhi. She had come out of the self-imposed political isolation at a time when the Congress faced an existential crisis. Regional satraps within the party were parting ways with the Congress. Loyalists within the party implored Gandhi to salvage the Congress. She finally came out and did a remarkable job to turnaround the fortunes of her party. She retrieved the Congress in late 1990s. After shedding the fat, the Congress sprung back strongly under her stewardship. She proved later that the Gandhi dynasty was not yet done with in the Indian politics. She led the Congress with grace. She was combative. She showed beautiful combination of grace and combativeness in the Indian politics. She never spoke extempore. But her speeches were well written and concise with punches, which she delivered in her trademark style.

She was no novice in politics when she was pulled into the Congress by 'orphaned' party old horses. She had run backroom office of the Congress when Rajiv Gandhi was alive. She knew the ways of politics and compulsions and weaknesses of the Congress leaders. She was well aware of the deep roots of the Congress in India. Even if the tree sheds all its leaves, its roots are potent enough to bring the green cover back. She knew well, that the people believed her party was congenitally blessed with power. People in India have an emotional bond with the Congress. That demography of India has changed, with 50 per cent of the population under the age of 29, is not a condition which should handicap the Congress to seek an alternative way for revival. The party has structure across the country. And that is quite an envious asset for any political outfit.

Sonia Gandhi as a politician was at her best to pick Manmohan Singh to lead India even while she held a tight grip over the Congress. It's to her credit that the Congress did not face more exoduses of leaders during her times. She did not disturb the status quo within the Congress, which served her well. But her son is different. He lacks abilities to deliver speeches extempore, but that would not hold him back in trying so. His tryst with extempore speeches has been made into hilarious videos shared on WhatsApp by the Congress leaders. They wonder the road ahead of the Congress under him. The older generation within the Congress has not much of hope from him. But they cannot do anything, because they know well that the Sonia Gandhi era is in its last leg and her son taking over the party is inevitable.

Gandhi is arguably a non-believer in the core character of the Congress of being a status-quoist party. He has had his own share of experiments within the party. His experiments left disastrous trails in the Congress. He brought American ideas of preliminaries, which made his party workers searing at each other. Even when the 2014 battle was a couple of years away he was actually thinking of Mission 2019. He is of the belief that his experiments would take time to bear fruits. He seeks to bring a new generation of leaders into the Congress. He was partially successful in 2009 when a few of his hand-picked young men and women were elected to the Lok Sabha and others to various state Assemblies. His critics slammed him for not speaking on issues. He had been a back-bencher in the Lok Sabha. Until his first speech in the 16th Lok Sabha on the issue of agrarian distress on accounts of unnseasonal rains and hailstorms, he had spoken twice in the Lower House in his over decade long parliamentary career. Afterwards, he has emerged as a 'Zero Hour' speaker in the Lok Sabha. After the Question Hour, scribes used to vacate the press gallery in the Lok Sabha, but now they stay perched at their respective seats in anticipation of him taking up an issue.

The Congress is split between the two camps. The elders in the party want to extend the reign of Sonia to the maximum. The younger lots, who sense an opportunity to climb up the ladder fast in leadership, want Rahul to assume the reign of the party at the earliest. The regional satraps within the Congress are ready to jump off the boat if Rahul were to become the president of the Party. And, knowing well the prospects, the Congress Working Committee extended tenure of Sonia by one more year. Rahul will have to wait much longer to get the mantle of the party leadership and till then he would have to live in the shadow of his mother.

The BJP is well aware of the consequences of Gandhi's bid to transform his image. The response of the Modi government on Gandhi's raising of issues in the 'Zero Hour' has been panicky to speak the least given the manner in which ministers after ministers give lengthy responses just after he sits down. The manner in which the Modi government joins the issue raised by Gandhi has been disproportionate. Within days of his return from his 56 days long sabbatical, Gandhi has made headlines, with ministers' responses appearing as footnotes. If Gandhi were to finally discover abilities to connect with the people, there is every possibility of Modi government running into a strong Opposition irrespective of the fact that the Congress has just 44 MPs in the Lok Sabha. Gandhi, however, is not aware that India seeks to break free from the shackles in which politics of the previous century bound the country. The change of demography has made his ideologies obsolete. He romanticizes his anti-industry image. He seeks to project a perception that a pro-industry government is sinful. He cannot wriggle himself out of his land acquisition politics. He wants to bind land owners to farming. His disconnect with India's farming population is self-evident. Marginal farmers have become construction labourers in places much near to the Tughlaq Lane residence of Gandhi.

India's farming population is indebted and various surveys have authoritatively stated that farmers are deeply in the grip of informal money-lenders in rural areas. Corporate farming in India has been a non-starter. The Cooperative farming may be the way out, but for it to become successful the dependent population on agriculture must come down by half at least in the next one and a half decades. Gandhi needs to get his economics correct if he at all wants to connect with the young India.

The 2014 verdict marked an end of the era of anti-Congressism in Indian politics. In the emergence of strong leadership under Modi, his opponents are seeking to unveil anti-BJPism. The Congress is much weaker and is likely to shed more weight in the coming years. Provincial leaders have begun making moves to unveil unified banner to stay relevant.

Gandhi has not yet the stature to fill the Opposition vacuum. The void will be filled in natural courses. As of now Nitish Kumar is a strong contender to fill the void. He has a stature and administrative experience to become a credible face of the Opposition. But he is pinned down in Bihar and has too many rivals within the socialist block who want him to fail in his immediate challenges. After disastrous electoral war with Modi, Kumar sought to salvage himself by floating the idea of uniting all offshoots of Janata Parivar into one political outfit. He took inspiration from the fact that the BJP was decimated in state elections in Delhi at the hands of Arvind Kejriwal of Aam Admi Party in a one on one fight.

A day before the 2008 Delhi Assembly verdict, Arun Jaitely had showed his flamboyant confidence of wining hands down the elections to a few journalists at Pant Marg state unit party office. The then state unit party chief Harsh Vardhan was in his company. For an hour, Jaitely took names of constituencies in Delhi where his party was winning. As he chatted on and on, Vardhan dozed off. Later, Vardan would show his tired and fatigued faces. None of Jaitely's flamboyance had any effect on Vardhan. The BJP was routed by the Congress, which was led by charismatic Sheila Dikshit in that elections. The BJP in Delhi has been treated by Jaitely as his fiefdom. After Madan Lal Khurana faded away from the Delhi politics, the BJP in the national capital has not yet found a leader who could appeal to the people. Dikshit's one and a half decades long rule gave telling blows to leadership of not only the BJP but the Congress also. Both the national parties suffer from leadership void.

Delhi also hosted Anna Hazare agitation. Even after the agitation withered away, its leftover in the form of Arvind Kejriwal and his company had enough head-start to challenge the mighty Dikshit. People in Delhi have paradoxical cynicism. They would break all rules. They would run down all in political class as scoundrels. More than half of Delhi's population lives in areas, which are unauthorized, where colonies came up by throwing all rule books to the wind. Delhi is a city of traders, property dealers, babus, and those who live off through rental incomes. They would want all luxury in their lives, but would not want to pay for services. In summers, they would have air-conditioners running in their homes, but would like electricity to be subsidized by tax payers' money. Women would be so lazy that they would drop their bags through ropes to vegetable vendors from their balconies and would not take pain to visit shops or markets. Yet, they would beat their chests for soaring vegetable prices.

Politics in Delhi is limited to issues of electricity and water bills and 'soaring' vegetable prices. Kejriwal was naturally suited to be a leader of such cynical snobs. Dikshit gave Delhi its garlands of flyovers and wide roads, which allow people to zip through in their swanky vehicles, while showing off their wealth. She expanded the network of drinking water pipelines to nook and corner of the national capital. Yet, she was rejected by people in a manner as if she had been a curse to the city.

Kejriwal did succeed in puncturing the Modi balloon which was floating on the horizon. The BJP had won all seven Lok Sabha seats in Delhi by huge margins. The BJP won state elections in Maharashtra, Haryana, and Jharkhand after the 2014 Lok Sabha elections. The party seemed unstoppable. Amit Shah's 'Ashwamedh' horse was let loose. The BJP was in an expansionist mode. The party was making lots of noise in new frontiers like West Bengal where the BJP had no footprints.

The BJP was not sure of Delhi. It kept delaying elections in the national capital. And by the time the BJP opted for elections, euphoria about Modi had considerably subsided and reality had struck people that the new Prime Minister was not a magician. People had good memories of Kejriwal's 49 days long government in the national capital. They believed that the petty corruption and Kejriwal do not co-exist. They were reeling under 'huge' electricity and water bills. Kejriwal promised to substantially take care of their burdens. He did take care of the concerns, as within days of coming to power he announced to subsidize the bills. Kejriwal's unprecedented electoral feat, which saw the Congress routed and the BJP decimated in Delhi, did a world of good to the Modi government. The arrogance of the Modi Cabinet sobered and political shrill with which the BJP had hit the trails in West Bengal subsided. Talks of Ashwamedha horse of the BJP let loose too stopped. The government began making amends with ruling parties in key states. Prime Minister broke the ice with West Bengal chief Minister Mamata Banerjee. He also began talking to Bihar chief minister Nitish Kumar. Irony of the state of polity was such that chief minister of West Bengal did not feel it proper even to speak to the Prime Minister of the country. Credit must go to Kejriwal that the jolt he gave to the BJP in the Delhi elections somehow triggered a patch up between the ruling NDA at the Centre and the regional parties in states, which in a way allowed Parliament to function in the most productive manner in the Budget session in 2015. Parliament could pass significant number of key legislation because of the support of the regional parties, which happened primarily because Modi made special efforts to reach out to Banerjee and Kumar by lapping the opportunity by both hands presented to him at private functions.

Kejriwal is a self-limiting activist turned politician. He was in the company of ultra-activists who thought that Delhi experiments could be replicated across the nation. Harsh reality, however, is that India is hardly just Delhi, and people have much more issues to worry about than paying bills of electricity and water. This dawned upon Kejriwal when he sweated in the summer of 2014 while contesting against Modi from Varanasi Lok Sabha constituency. A vast majority of people in states in fact do not even pay electricity and water bills, which proved detrimental to the acceptance of Kejriwal elsewhere in the country. The acerbic negativism which afflicted India during the UPA-II is also no more around to provide Kejriwal a congenial environment to grow and play a role at the national level. He borrowed the idea of his politics from West Bengal when in heydays of Left rule the CPI (M) had a network of 'mohalla committees' in nook and corner. He conveniently got rid of all his associates who had national ambitions. Kejriwal is largely another regional leader or a leader of a glorified municipality who has carved out his territory.

There are arguably two leaders who have another two decades of politics left in them with potential to play a larger role at the national level. They are Nitish Kumar and Akhilesh Yadav. Sections of the BJP had given Kumar the certificate of a Prime Minister material before Modi arrived on the national scene. He is not a mass leader in the league of Modi. But he has many admirers within the regional block. His stature makes him stay in the media limelight. When he speaks, he is heard with all seriousness. He is blessed with a lot of common sense. But he chose to go back into the socialist block where personal ego and caste identity are too strong for leaders to come together for a bigger cause. Kumar caught national attention when he with the support of the BJP ended the Lalu Prasad-Rabri Devi rule in Bihar. For over eight years, his politics in Bihar was to banish even the shadow of Prasad. The irony of politics is that he became chief minister of Bihar another time with the help of Prasad after snapping ties with the BJP. The level of distrust within the Janata Parivar constituents whose unification Kumar seeks is such that his regular dinner meeting with Jaitely is considered reason enough for provincial leaders to keep distance from him.

Akhilesh Yadav in 2012 was sworn in as India's youngest ever chief minister. He has seen three painful years of woeful administration in which he had been pulled in different directions by a brigade of uncles. The 2014 electoral rout was a blessing in disguise for him to shrug off unnecessary shadows. He has gained experience and is now a leader by all accounts. He too is a provincial leader, but has an advantage of his state Uttar Pradesh having 80 Lok Sabha seats, which is double than any large state. He does not have a national stature like Kumar, but has the potential to acquire one. His party because of the sheer size of Uttar Pradesh will be a natural choice to lead any formation of regional parties against Modi.

Regional parties are not facing leadership crisis. They are firmly placed in Uttar Pradesh, Bihar, West Bengal, Odisha, Telangana, Andhra Pradesh, and Tamil Nadu. These states have almost half of the total strength of the Lok Sabha. The Congress has been decimated in all these states and recovery there would be too daunting in the near future. Regional parties in these states will nonetheless have to face the rise of the BJP in their backyards. The BJP has a few more frontiers like the

North-east, Odisha, and West Bengal to make significant gains in near future.

Economy is poised for significant bounce. The economic growth is back on seven plus percentage growth trajectory. There is major public investment taking place in Railways, which has potential to add even two percentage points in national Gross Domestic Product (GDP). The infrastructure sector, including mining, power generation, road construction, urbanization, is gaining pace. They have the potential to significantly spur the GDP growth, besides generating millions of jobs.

The GDP growth of eight percentages and more is within the sight. There is every possibility that Modi's last three years in office (2016-19) could see the GDP growth of nine per cent or more. Industrial expansion is on the card. 'Make in India' is being talked about at every forum. His government is gearing to pump in billions of dollars in asset creation in irrigation infrastructure. Modi is apparently scripting fundamental change in India's policy towards poor of the country. For over six decades, India's identity had been of a welfare state. Modi believes that there had been a caucus who laid siege to the national exchequer in the name of welfare programmes and looted the country. He is arguably correct also.

Enabling is the buzz word in the scheme of things of Modi. It is early days to make any definite view on the direction of the economy, but signs are clear that India under Modi is making a transition from a welfare state to an enabling one. Modi seeks to provide an enabling environment for businesses to flourish. He wants to enable the youth to become entrepreneurs. He wants to enable the farmers to make a transition to better lives with modern tools and knowledge. He seeks to enable poor of the country to tap the banking platform for social security. He ensured that more than 100 million bank accounts were opened for those who had no banking access. Through insurance and pension schemes wherein the poor would pour in their contributions, Modi is seeking to enable them to provide for their own social security.

Modi's sanguine focus on infrastructure development is also in line with his zeal to provide enabling facilities for India to emerge one single economic entity and market. The Goods and Services Tax (GST) is aimed to enable India to emerge a single market entity. The move will address the inherent distortions, which make businesses and movement of goods cumbersome. If Modi succeeds in scripting transition of India from a welfare state to an enabling state, he will leave too strong footprints for the posterity. The move will invite strong backlash, but Modi has shown signs of being equally combative to take head on his adversaries.

It is early days to sight 'Achhe Din' in India. But there is one aspect, which is clearly seen in full force and that is drying up of black money generation in few pockets. Delhi and its adjoining areas had been booming real-estate market, which thrived in pumping of black money. Even while the economy was stressed the real-estate market stayed unscathed. In one year of Modi in the office, roughly the real estate prices in Delhi and adjoining cities have slumped by at least 20 per cent. This is a sign worth scrutiny. The economy is back on track, but the real estate prices are slipping. This is arguably a good omen. It affirms that Modi's war cry 'naa khaaoonga, naa khane doons (neither will I be corrupt nor would I let others be), which he delivered from the ramparts of Red Fort in 2014, is bearing fruits. And if it does succeed to bear fruits, India will cut through the cancer of corruption in all walks of lives to become a stronger nation.

To the credit of Modi, he is a tough task master and monitors the works quite minutely. Ever since he became Prime Minister, Modi has been holding monthly review meetings of infrastructure sector wherein he takes stock of progress on tasks with timeline set in previous meetings and hammers out bottlenecks right there which impede progress. Modi is a compulsive political campaigner. He has no faith in the saying, 'the wise speaks less'. His image is that of a globe-trotter, with fascination to address Indian Diaspora. He addresses Non-Resident Indians, but ends up sending political messages to domestic audiences. The fact that NRIs had not elected him to the post of Prime Minister nor would they ever do so does not bother him. Audiences in various countries have heard his long form of oratory.

He may arguably be the first Prime Minister who never shies away from making political comments on foreign soil. He is well aware of the fact that he is a politician in a television age. He may be speaking on foreign soil, but his speeches are heard by millions of people back home. He's building a cult around him. He's not alone in doing so, as many of his predecessors have done. He's well aware of the fact that there were a few achievements of Manmohan Singh government too, which could not get communicated. Modi is a marketing wizard, who can magnify even his small achievements to look grand. He knows if he talks less, others will talk more. He also knows that his talks are getting repetitive. He knows that substance of his talks would come from achievements of his government. He's also aware of the fact that mere talking about achievements would not be enough until people could relate with them. There will need to be visible changes on the ground.

Modi harvested groundswell of support for him across the nation. India awaits groundswell of positive feedback for development. The Modi era has begun. History will record its length.

ABOUT THE AUTHOR

MANISH ANAND is a New Delhi based political journalist. He has extensively travelled length and breadth of the country. He works for The Asian Age newspaper. He has been covering politics for over a decade. He covers proceedings of the Indian Parliament for his newspaper. Previously, he worked for The Statesman.

He's also a regular commentator on India's foreign affairs. Besides politics, Manish keenly follows key ministries of India's Central government. He has closely followed the affairs of the Congress, BJP, and socialist parties. He saw from close quarters the functioning of the decade long Manmohan Singh led UPA government.